ATTRACT

ACTIVATE THE 4X SYSTEM TO ATTRACT LISTINGS AND BUYERS

Tracy

Here is a little gift for you. I hope there are some nuggets here that help.

Great meeting you and reconnecting today

Kelly

KELLY JOHNSTON

CREATOR OF THE 4X FORMULA REAL ESTATE BUSINESS SERIES

Prominence Publishing www.prominencepublishing.com

The Author can be reached as follows:
Kelly Johnston
kelly@4Xformula.com
www.4Xformula.com
Twitter: https://twitter.com/4x_real
Instagram: https://www.instagram.com/realestate.with.kelly/ or @realestate.with.kelly
Facebook: @KellyJohnston.Training
LinkedIn: https://www.linkedin.com/in/4xformula/
YouTube: Type in 4XFormula Real Estate Training in the search bar
Podcasts – On all the platforms look for 4XFormula Radio

ATTRACT/Johnston, Kelly. -- 1st ed.

ISBN: 978-1-988925-81-3

CONTENT

About the Author	5
What to Expect From This Book	7
The Four Pillars of Real Estate Success	13
The 4X Formula.	22
The Dream Business	24
The Start – Starting right	33
The Mental State of Success	34
Let's get Started!	40
Goal Setting for Real Estate	46
The 9 Facets of the 4X Agent	59
The 9 Facets to Becoming a Complete 4X Agent	61
The 4X Agent's 12 Points of Power	66
Four Mindshifts for New Real Estate Agents	68
Mindset Mastery, Part One	76
Mindset Mastery, Part Two	99
Quick Commission Blueprint	113
The Art of the Conversation	137
Get Listings	154
The Separation is in the Preparation	178
The Pre-Listing Interview	187

Master of the Open House 196
Marketing Strategies Leading up to the Open House 205
The Seven Stages of Contact 214
Neighbourhood Specialist 232
Mindshare 242
The Attractor Factor 248
Preview of Book 2 – ATTAIN 254
Conclusion and WHAT'S NEXT? 268
TOOLS 274

ABOUT THE AUTHOR

Kelly Johnston is just a regular person like you. His approach to the training program is meant to relate to all levels of real estate professionals and to ensure that he gives more value to the agent than expected. It is a complete course that covers all aspects of attracting clients to building long-term success in the real estate business.

He and his wife, Nicole, still work as licensed real estate professionals. This information is up to date and can be applied in today's market — right now. While writing and marketing the 4X Formula Real Estate Course and producing the FREE content and podcast episodes, he and his wife still manage to average 6 to 9 deals per month in their business, earning six figures in commissions consistently since its inception. Kelly and Nicole love to travel and to go camping. They have fiercely loyal clients and find that over 80% of their new business is coming from referrals.

Kelly has been a licensed professional since 1997 and Nicole joined him after their youngest son, Landon, started going to school full time in 2010. Kelly has received a minimum of at least one commission cheque monthly (at times they have enjoyed over 20 commission cheques in a month) without missing a month, since 2003. That is a statistic that very few real estate agents can match. Their success is predicated on the systems that are taught in the 4X Formula Real Estate Mastery Course. Kelly first began working on the course when he discovered the formula, after years of frustration, in 2015. Kelly has organized and managed larger teams as well as owned and operated Real Estate Brokerages over the last two decades. He has also recruited and trained many agents over the years. He found that a lot of training and coaching programs were missing the "building block" approach. In his own business and Real Estate brokerage, he found he did not have the time to create a proper training program that allowed new agents to thrive from "mini-successes" nor build up their businesses, in a defined and intentional way. It had to be created. After years of reading many books, listening to CD's, podcasts, going to seminars, and paying for training from other top Real Estate guru's, Kelly believes that he has designed a course that fills in the gaps and hopefully becomes another trusted training program that Real Estate offices all over North America will implement.

Finally, after 5 years of development and testing with other agents, we can deliver this information to you in an organized and functional format.

WHAT TO EXPECT FROM THIS BOOK

This book is for you. If you are new in the real estate business—or if you'd just like to leap up to a new level of success—this book is dedicated to you.

You may be newly licensed. You may be an agent who has been in the business long enough to run out of their first sphere of influence, circle of friends and family and are now struggling to get listings and meet new prospective clients. You may be a successful agent who wants to build a team of people who do all of the correct activities with the correct mindsets. No matter where you are in your real estate career, you're going to want to have a copy of *Attract* in your real estate toolkit.

My hope is that this book will be around long enough to become a staple in real estate offices, to inspire their new agents with strategies that get results.

I find that there is a lot of time wasted in the beginning months when agent/brokers are simply learning "what to do." Not to mention, training the new recruits is time-consuming for real estate owners. As of this writing, statistics claim that 87% of the agents who get licensed are out of the business within two to three years. That leaves 13% making real estate into a living, a worthy career, or a 'side hustle.' 20% of that group will go on to make great money and become well-known agents in their marketplace. Visualize this: I have 100 people; 87 leave the business leaving 13 to carry on....and out of that 13, only two and a half people make a proper living at it. Just over 2 people out of 100! What a daunting stat!

Flipping this statistic is one of the main reasons I've written this book. It is also the driving factor behind my 4X Formula Real Estate training course.

Here are a few scenarios that new agents unwittingly walk into when they begin their real estate careers. I do not intend to disparage any real estate office or their business models. I was an owner/broker too and I am well aware of the challenges. That is not my point here. I am simply pointing out how it seems when someone begins their career in Real Estate. There are many offices that create a wonderful environment for their agents. To be truthful, I hope that my book can help Real Estate Office Broker /Owners get their new agents started correctly. You may relate to one or more of these:

1. "*Here is your desk*" or, "*Here is your workstation. Good Luck.*"

Make sure your fees are paid every month. After that, it is expected that you will now learn by osmosis. You might get some answers if you ask the right questions. The rest is up to you. Training will happen on the fly, as you learn how to do your paperwork, how you can stay onside with the legal ramifications that might arise. Your office manager will ensure that you write a proper contract to save him from having to answer to the legal codes to which real estate professionals adhere. That is their main concern.

2. *"All our new agents are paired up with a mentor."*

Your mentor will deal with the details involved with starting a real estate business. When your first listing happens, they will step in to help you prepare the paperwork. When you create an opportunity for an offer, then they help you with the details. You may get a few pointers from these people and learn about business building from these people. When you have an idea, they will help guide you to work within the realm of what is legal, ethical, and over-all acceptable. But step-by-step, tactical learning is not happening. There are no building blocks to the lessons you're learning; It is not systematic. The only wisdom a mentor can provide, normally, is whatever system worked for that mentor.

Often the mentor, in providing you with knowledge to get through your first layer of deals that may come to you from your first sphere of influence, will receive a large percentage of your first few sales. I have seen as high as 50% of your commissions. If your first two or three deals have an average total commission of $18,000, you might be losing as much as $9,000 to your mentor, a figure you'll have to accept as "just a cost of doing business."

3. *"Professional training provided by the office is part of our onboarding for new agents."*

Fantastic. If the office has a great training program, designed to help you obtain business quickly with detailed, systematic steps and provide the materials and tools that make you look like a rock star, then you are in a fantastic office. If accountability measures and team coaching are in place, then that is going to help you.

But be careful: Office training will either work for you or it will not. Depending on the culture of the office, you will either thrive in the new environment or wither away. For example, if the training is predicated upon knocking on doors, cold calling for leads and getting trained on scripts, then some of you will flounder. If the training subject matter is focused on either motivating you on to pump you up, or shaming you for not succeeding, one of two things will occur: You'll be pumped up and become one of the few who make it, or you'll be deflated, and become a statistic.

4. *You begin as a team member for a top-producing agent.*

This is a great opportunity for you, as long as you use it as a launch pad for your own business. If you are happy to work for someone else's dream, and enjoy the structure, security and lifestyle of that arrangement, then so be it.

On the other hand, if you want to control your own destiny and grow a business that organically sustains itself and grows, then you will eventually have to leave the nest. If you are paying 50% of your commission to a listing agent, that is a great leverage point for that senior agent. It can also be a great leverage point for you. There is a sense of security that comes from knowing that you are working daily and getting paid. You can learn about serving people. You will learn how to communicate clearly and how to negotiate deals. The experience of a senior agent can be a very positive influence on you. However, there will come a time where you will have to take what you need from that experience and build your own business; otherwise, you will always be beholden to that person. Working for yourself is a position you'll want to get to if you want to be in the top 20%.

If you like the idea of minimal expenses, and your current office has a good, respectful, working atmosphere that is a good fit for you, then I am excited for you. That is totally okay.

However, for those of you who want to build your own business and brand, I have a plan for you.

I know that I have only touched on four different types of office styles. There are many more but the ones I've mentioned in this book are the most typical. There are some amazing boutique firms out there that are structured specifically for their market and the demographic they serve. For example, some offices are created solely for a developer to market their own product. But let's all agree on this: All new real estate agents have to take a course and pass an exam, to qualify to become a licensed real estate professional. No matter where you are in North America, the course is similar in subject matter, with only slight variations concerning legal terms, and different ways titles are registered, etc. But, I think that you will agree that the course that you take to become *licensed* does not teach you how to *succeed* in real estate. I can state with a perfect confidence that the people who write the licensing courses have never succeeded in real estate.

The next challenge is that there is no "one size fits all" approach to success for every single real estate professional. There are so many variables: personality, life experience, past work experience; marketing experience. And then there are specific markets, office culture, and the ever-changing influence of social media. Then, add to that, the turbulent world in which we live: natural disasters, viral pandemics, terrorist attacks, stock market crashes, government policy changes, the effect of immigration, interest rates, lending rules and policies, technological advances.

In your community, a new business may set up and hire a lot of people or a major employer may shut down due to changes in how people buy, sell, or utilize a product, leaving 100's or even 1000's of people suddenly jobless. There are multiple outside influences that can affect our business of real estate.

The only way to combat the chaos is to focus on the fundamentals of business building. Focus on what you can control. There are many things that will occur in your marketplace which aren't in your control. My goal is to empower you to thrive, no matter the situation.

Treat your real estate career as a business and build it: learn and apply, tweak, learn and apply, tinker, learn and apply. Find what works for you and find what doesn't. If a certain skill is necessary but you don't have it, find someone else who is good at it, then hire them. The alternative is to learn that skill and master it. I am going to teach you the skills that will empower you to build your own future, and increase your presence, your expertise, your reputation, and your brand, without spending money unnecessarily.

There are many ways to create a successful real estate business, but the fundamentals will always hold true. There are many training styles out there. There are many coaching programs. There are many books to read, and yet, here you are with a copy of *Attract* in your hand (or maybe on your Phone!).

Thank you for joining me on this journey. My hope is that you utilize this book as a sort of manual to refer back to. I hope it inspires you to become a member of the 4X Formula System so that you leave "no holes in the bucket." My goal is to leave nothing to chance. I wrote this book hoping that this book will serve you in creating a solid plan for your business to ATTRACT Listings. There are three more books in the works right now that coincide with the remaining pillars of the 4X Formula Real Estate Course.

THE FOUR PILLARS OF REAL ESTATE SUCCESS

It is my over-arching goal, that a 4X Agent understand the power of the four pillars: **ATTRACT, ATTAIN, SERVE, and RETAIN.** If you are fully competent in all these areas, you will never be looking for business. Leads and listings will fill your inbox. There will be a constant flow of business coming your way. You will experience paying deals every single month, like I have for nearly two decades. Here is how it breaks down:

ATTRACT.

It is important to know how to get business. This comes first, attract listings and buyers. Once these skills are mastered, you will always know how to get business when you need to. The real estate business is not consistent. There are many variables. However, I will contest that there is opportunity in any market. If it is a buyer's market, there is opportunity. If it is a seller's market, there is opportunity. If it is a balanced market, there is opportunity. There is always opportunity. Uncovering where the easiest and most profitable business is hiding is a skill that we will cover in this book. Mastering the ability to attract the best leads to grow your business quickly is incredibly empowering. Once you have mastered this, you can move to any city in North America and, with confidence, build a successful business. [Check out my podcast 4XFSO2E11 "Build A Business That You Love..." where I interview Matt Kuchar. He is a prime example of someone who has mastered the art of attracting business]. The truth is, you may know a lot of people, you may enjoy people. This may be one of the fundamental reasons that you thought that Real Estate would be a good career for you, and that is wonderful. Your sphere of influence is just the start, and it is the bonus business that may come to you once in a while. You must master the art of Attracting business to you on a daily basis. The premise that I created this concept from is this "what if, scenario":

> *I am a licensed Real Estate Professional. I get on a plane in California. As the plane is flying across the continent, I jump out of the plane, and wherever I land is where I now build my business. I have enough money for four months of lodging and food. No friends. No family. No past jobs. No past sports teams. No connections in this new community. No bonus business.*
>
> *What would I do?*

This is the premise of ATTRACT.

ATTAIN.

You are now constantly creating opportunities to meet sellers and buyers to engage in business with you. This is what you do. Your job is to meet people. Attaining the business, or "Winning the Business," is your next skill. The key here is to increase your "dollar per hour" by becoming highly skilled at converting leads to listings. Here is the ultimate process, as I see it, for every LEAD:

LEAD **to** Contact **to** Contract **to** Commission **to** Raving Fan **to** Referral Source **to** Future Business.

When you attract buyers, you multiply your efforts. This is crucial to your exponential success. Your ability to ATTAIN the business, once you ATTRACT the opportunities, will increase over time, and that increases your conversion rates, which increases your $/Time output or your dollar per Hour. We touch on those skills in *Attract*, but we dig deeper into those skills in my next book, *Attain*.

There is a systematic approach for everything. Then you add your personality style to the process and make it yours. The key element that I want you to achieve in this section is to have full confidence in all situations to be able to ATTAIN or WIN the business. When you are on the phone, from a *sign call* (someone sees your listing sign and calls), you will convert that person into a buyer if they are not already working with another agent. By dealing with email inquiries or internet leads that come to you from your website, you will learn the skills to win their business. When you get a call for a listing appointment, you will show up for that meeting with confidence that you will win that listing on your terms. I know that if I have a chance to meet someone face-to-face, in their home, I will win the business if it is meant to be. It is a rare occurrence when someone meeting multiple agents doesn't choose me to list their home. It's very rare because I have learned the skillsets from 24 years of trial and error, and I have a fully developed value proposition. In my marketplace, I know that there are certain agents who try everything they can to get that person to sign the listing contract before meeting me because they're afraid that if they allow that person to meet me, they will not be selected. That is what you want for your dream real estate business.

SERVE.

This is where we celebrate the power of the servant and of service. When we serve people well—when we "Wow" them—we create a lasting impression that creates a ripple effect for more business. Serving clients unconditionally creates the impression that you went above and beyond your job to create the best possible result for them. We have created tools for this and systems that will not only help you do a great job, but also instill in your clients the feeling that you, the agent, have everything under control. Your goal is to create fans who will send business your way. Invest in this instead of big billboards and bus bench ads and you will be amazed at how easily business will come to you.

This is the point where you begin to plant seeds of greatness so that, eventually, you will reap what you sow. From attracting the client, to meeting the client, to attaining the business, to serving the client, to the after-sales service; there is always a process, a system, a formula. Do this well, and you will never be looking for business. Some clients are more difficult than others. We allow for this. Your attitude is a big factor in the success of this Third Pillar. Treat every client as if they are worth over $75,000 to your business and notice how your attitude shifts. By the way, they are worth it.

RETAIN.

Your existing business, and your past business, and the new leads that are in your pipeline, are all equally important. When people get all caught up in the "busy-ness" of their business, they tend to sacrifice other parts of the process that feed their success. One habit to building a successful business that feeds you for decades is client retention. A business that constantly produces more business is the absolute goal. You want to create an organic business that feeds itself.

We work so hard to ATTRACT...then we put a lot of work, time, and effort into ATTAINING the business; then, once we win the business, we work so hard at SERVING people well. The final step is to RETAIN the client's loyalty. By osmosis, we nurture the client's confidence in us; a confidence that we can provide a service. I am here to tell you that you need to continue to earn their business and earn the right to be referred. My final book, *RETAIN*, contains some of the most important lessons of all. The great thing about RETAIN is that it works. There is a huge leverage point here that helps you continue to receive business from your database.

So…can you see how important all four pillars are to realizing true real estate success?

Become a 4X Agent.

There is a misunderstanding in common thought that stems from how we observe other people and ascertain what "success" looks like. I believe that a real estate agent who has all four pillars in order can experience what I refer to as The Dream Business. I will talk about the Dream Business in a future chapter. I call my real estate students "4X Agents," or "4X'ers". My goal is to create an army of 4X'ers, all skilled at all Four Pillars, operating in the marketplace and building a reputation that impacts our industry in a positive way. That is my dream.

There are a lot of agents we see operating in our markets right now. Some are on TV. Some have big teams with billboards on bus benches and magazine ads. They have a bunch of Instagram followers. Most of the time, they look like they should be touring the modelling circuit. They drive fancy cars. They wear expensive clothing. They have personal trainers at the gym. They are amazing and beautiful and, on the outside, seem like they are the picture of success that we need to achieve.

I will tell you this: Half of the time, these are 1X or 2X Agents, not 4X Agents. Something is being sacrificed. I watch the Million Dollar Listing agents on those TV shows and I notice the conversations they have. I see how they talk about their clients behind their backs. It may be good drama…but even those who are "highly successful" do not have a confident control of the process. They are operating out of desperation, for the commission. They are not leading their clients.

They are a pawn in their clients' game. But it's good TV, I suppose. They need the drama to keep it interesting.

Let's take it down a notch and look at a top producer, one who may be in your office right now, or at least in your direct market area. Check out that agent's business. Do they have a lot of listings? Are a lot of those listings over-priced? Do they have an inventory that is all over the map? Do you hear them complain about their clients all the time? Do they seem frantic and out of control? Are they processing a lot of deals? Are they spending a lot of money on advertising to attract strangers? Do you see any weaknesses in their processes?

Take a closer look. Is it frustrating to deal with them? Are they difficult to contact? When you send an offer to them, does it take them four to six hours to get back to you? Go to one of their open houses. Check out their marketing materials. What do their photos look like? Does that agent rely too heavily on their administration person for everything so that vital details get overlooked? Is their admin person ready for the loony bin because he/she is so stressed out?

Maybe more cracks are showing: their listing data is incorrect because they don't update their listing information properly or in a timely manner; their whole contact management system is in a database, but nobody ever gets a phone call; their sellers only hear from the admin person and never the actual listing agent unless an offer comes in or it is time to renew the listing contract

Perhaps they have a buyer's agent who sells all of the buyers' homes, so, they never meet these people. Yet, they feel entitled to the listing when the buyer chooses to sell in a couple of years, despite never having met them!

At this top real estate office, the focus is completely on "the GETTING" of business. They know how to ATTRACT. It's called being skilled at "Self Promotion." They are very skilled at attracting strangers to get the phone to ring. In addition, they may be highly skilled at ATTAINING the business. Some people have a natural ability to sell themselves to others. Sound fair?

Where these top producers fail is in the SERVE and RETAIN area. So, as a result, they are forced to completely focus on ATTRACT and ATTAIN all the time. Each meeting to ATTAIN the business is with strangers that they have to 'convince and sell' their services to. If this person goes on a vacation, many times, these LEADS will not wait for them. That lead will move on to the next agent. This agent understands and accounts for this. Is this The Dream Business? In my opinion, no. This is a 2X Agent.

SERVE and RETAIN are being sacrificed. These real estate entities are all about the machine and keeping it fed. Their complete focus is to ensure that leads keep coming in so that they can get more business. This is common. I relate to this because that is the business I created years ago. I know what was happening under the surface. I know the internal stresses that are being experienced. I know the truth. It took me a long time to admit it, but once I truly understood the mess that I created and admitted to the amount of money that was flowing away from me, I knew I had to make some changes.

We look at these people and see them as extremely successful. They might be. It depends on whatever measuring stick is used to determine success. What goes overlooked is a sense of enormous insecurity that can develop due to the fear that builds up. Costs keep coming in every month. Did you know that carrying a lot of Listings can become a major liability if they don't sell?

Maybe other aspects of the agent's life are being sacrificed. I know an agent who is extremely successful. She has two nannies looking after her daughter and a team of people with two assistants. She is smart and very capable. Do you see where one part of her life is being sacrificed? But she is known as the #1 Agent in Canada for her company.

Years ago, I had a team of four people, one full-time staffer, and a few service providers that I paid monthly so that I could handle the volume. I referred to us as "the machine." It's a machine that needs fuel. The fuel is money. I remember constantly wondering where all my money was going. I had a "million dollar" business and was maybe retaining about $250K out of that, once everybody got their share. Everyone else was getting 50% or more, and I was left with a meager 25% after the dust settled and I was the one paying for everything!! I was working 60 to 70 hours a week and had no life. Then, on top of all that, my "teammates" were busy building their own businesses on my dime!! Then they went out and became my competition! Does that sound like a DREAM BUSINESS?

Yet...this is what is taught by the big training and coaching gurus out there. I see it in many popular training programs aimed at real estate agents. What I have just described is their business model. So, it makes sense to sell the highest ticket offering, right? Think about it: If they show you how to earn $1 Million then it is easy for you to justify paying me $10,000 to $40,000 to learn how to make that $1 million, right? But is it still worth it if you only NET $250,000? Maybe? That's up to you.

But 2X Agents will continue to fight for business constantly. It's a never-ending cycle that will only intensify. I know... because I did what they taught. I got what I thought I wanted. What I was taught that I wanted. People thought I was successful. I made sure of that.

But when I look back on it now, I wasn't truly successful. There were so many things being sacrificed, and I was constantly in a state of stress. Think of it this way:

Picture a bathtub. You turn on the tap to fill the bathtub. Normally, there is enough hot water to fill the tub. But imagine if the plug just didn't quite make a proper seal and water was constantly draining out of the tub. I once rented a basement suite in my early years that had a tub like that. I could not take a bath. It was impossible; I would have to keep the water running the whole time and, eventually, the hot water would run out and cold water would start running into the tub.

In a very simplified way, this is a metaphor for 2X Agent business: a tub with a weak plug in it. Business is constantly draining out of the tub, so the tap has to be running, and eventually the hot water runs out, because the tap has to be turned on full blast.... constantly. That is your energy, money and time, running down the drain.

What if you built a business where you plugged those holes and actually saved yourself a lot of energy, money and time? EMT. These are your most valuable resources. What if you built a business where you just turned on the tap once in a while, when you needed to, and saved energy the rest of the time? This is what I call 4X'ing your business. Become a 4X Agent and utilize the 4X Formula and you can 4X your business. If you are expending EMT in a consistent way, wouldn't it be great to 4X those resources?

THE 4X FORMULA.

Now, imagine this....

What if you developed a real estate business that was extremely cost-effective, produced constant leads, attracted people that you enjoyed working with. Then, as you listed each property, you utilized the 4X Formula and turned each listing into four commission cheques. Leverage your EMT! List the Home, sell it. That Seller needs a home to Buy. Then ATTRACT two Buyers from that Listing. That is 4 Commission Cheques. That is the 4X Formula.

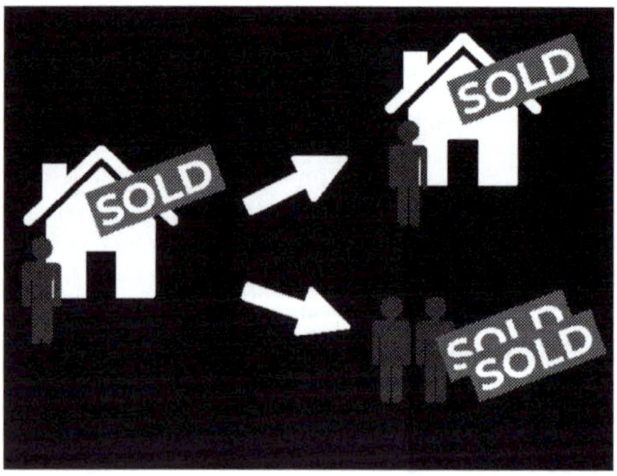

The next part of the formula would work like this. It is a known statistic from the National Association of REALTORs® that 50% of buyers have something to sell. So, every time you listed a home and worked on attracting two more buyers, the process would continue.

If you could focus intently and strategically on this formula, in everything that you do, while becoming a master of the Four Pillars: ATTRACT, ATTAIN, SERVE, and RETAIN. You'd be planting seeds for more business at the same time you were doing business, and you would never be concerned about LEADS coming to you. One of the greatest fears all real estate professionals face is, simply, running out of leads. So, with the 4X Formula, you simply create a lead cycle that feeds the business. It's a cycle that is constantly in motion.

All you need to do is employ the tactics and strategies that we teach in the Four Pillars, turn on the perpetual machine of the 4X Formula and then enjoy the DREAM BUSINESS.

THE DREAM BUSINESS

What is the DREAM BUSINESS? Well, this is worth talking about, huh?

This is a question that is subjective on so many levels but, if you'll indulge me, I will go over the main elements of the *DREAM Real Estate Business* and the lifestyle that comes along with it. You can agree or disagree with me, if you like. That is totally okay.

However, I would challenge you to write down what *you* visualise as your DREAM REAL ESTATE BUSINESS. Write out those above four words. Close your eyes and imagine the perfect real estate business and the perfect lifestyle for you and your loved ones. By the way, you have full license to change this vision over the years. That is your option, always. You grow, you learn, you adjust and tinker—and the net effect is that your mind is forced to open up and see new horizons. New possibilities. New Challenges. New Levels of Belief.

I wish this for you. I hope you allow this to happen in your life. Furthermore, I hope that *I* can be a positive influence on making this happen for you!!

Okay...here we go!

1. **Consistency.**

Consistent leads. Consistent listings. Consistent commission cheques. When you decided to make real estate your full-time profession, here is what you inadvertently chose to give up:

- A consistent paycheck from an employer.
- A budget based on your expected monthly income.
- Consistent working hours that are established by someone else.

In a word – Control.

You never know how long things will take with a client. The gestation period for each deal is totally inconsistent. From the day you meet someone who wants to employ your services to help them buy or sell, to the date that you actually *realize* a commission cheque is an unknown. The Crash of 2008 taught us that our system is fragile. COVID-19 has taught us that there is no way to predict anything. Every four years, a new president gets elected and, from the months leading up to that event and for a few months after the election occurs, we all seem to press PAUSE to see what happens. Natural disasters, like floods and hurricanes, can literally freeze all business in the affected areas for months and months...and sometimes years. It has become too normal for real estate agents to get so accustomed to uncertainty and inconsistency that they often operate in a state of constant insecurity. In fact, it becomes habitual to operate in a "topsy-turvy" lifestyle. This lifestyle is not sustainable and the stresses that are infused into your daily life will cause other issues. I have seen the negative consequences of that happen many times to others.

So, a stronger and more resilient business model is what we are working towards. It is not a quick process, but it is the goal and it can be accomplished. As of the writing of this book, I have been paid every single month in real estate, during all of the pandemics, market crashes and tragedies that have occurred in our world, for 18 years. I am still a real estate professional and have never been paid less than one commission cheque and as much as 20 commission cheques.

2. **Over 60% Referred**

Early on in the course, we go over goal setting for real estate. Part of that exercise is recording where our business comes from. Doing this habitually, helps in many ways and one of those ways is so you can see where you need to focus your efforts to maximize them. In order to create consistency in your business, you must nurture referrals and ensure that you receive "return business." There are tactics and strategies for this, but the magic to it all is how you conduct yourself during the transaction and after the transaction. How strong is the relationship that was built during the process?

The foundation to all relationship is trust. How do you build trust effectively and intentionally? The people you serve should be inspired to send people to you.

3. **Exceed the Goals**

We set goals based on certain criteria. We talk about *lead measures* and *lag measures*. Goals are set to give you a target for the year. Measuring the goals along the way is absolutely critical to your success. We have tools for this target right here, in the chapter of this book addressing Goal Setting. The Dream Business is one that exceeds our goals. We set stretch goals, based on foundational parameters, and then we are ready for the bonus business that comes to us from referrals, strategic alliances and return clients calling us suddenly, with no warning.

That is how you set, meet and then exceed your goals.

4. **Time OFF: No Effect on Business BUT Huge Effect on Lifestyle**

This sounds so simple, doesn't it? But it's not simple. It's a crucial element to the DREAM BUSINESS. Can you relate to this?

Most agents who are new in the business are so stressed that every single lead is momentous. Every single opportunity that they dig up or that just "comes" to them is extremely valuable. If they aren't there to answer that call or jump on that opportunity right when it comes, they're afraid they've lost their only chance.

We start with a restrictive consciousness and worry that we can lose business if we aren't available 100% of the time. Over time—after building quality relationships with new people or "unmet friends," as well as keeping connected with past clients—we begin to build a solid foundation of people that know, like and trust us. When that happens, we can say we have a solid business.

When you go off on a family camping trip for a few days, or if you take a two-week trip to an off-the-grid island, you will have the confidence to tell clients that you are not available and—here is the magic—they will wait for you! They will respect your personal time and be there to do business with you when you return. The reason for that is simple: You are who they want to deal with. They don't just want to settle for any real estate agent. They want to deal with you, and only you. That is the database that you want.

Taking time off to be with your loved ones is critical. Your kids need to see that you make being with your spouse, or significant other, one on one, a priority. That is a fantastic example to teach them. They need to see that, even though you work very hard and sometimes put in long hours, you make them your priority. If you have children, they need to see that you make them a priority as well. After all, why are you working so hard? For them, I hope. Your schedule must include supporting your kids, in their events, sports, dance, school functions, vacations together, and one-on-one time. This is crucial to living a balanced life.

In 2018, just three years after implementing what I now call the 4X Formula into my own life and business, I turned 50 years old. Here is what we managed to do outside of my real estate business that year. We went on multiple camping trips and attended every one of my son Connor's rugby and football games and practices. My wife Nicole and I volunteered at our church, working with the youth group on Wednesday nights and helping set up on Sunday morning services about two to three times per month. We travelled to Paris for a two-week vacation to celebrate my 50 years on this earth; we travelled to England with our two boys for two weeks to see my daughter who was attending university there. Nicole and I visited Cuba for a quick seven-day getaway to relax and do nothing. We enjoyed many more activities outside of real estate and still managed around 110 transactions. I earned over $550,000 that year. Time off had no effect on our production.

5. **NET more $**

In every business of any kind, we calculate *gross* Income and then *net* income. If you own a rental property, you want to know the net income after expenses to help you see if the mortgage payment can be paid out of those net proceeds. If you have ever been a business owner, you will know how important that net figure is. This is the number that matters.

I have been to Big Name training courses all over North America, and I watch the trainer bring up the successful agents who have been utilizing their systems, and I have to hear them brag about their production. But they never talk about the net figure.

The truth is, they probably don't really know. I totally relate to that. At the time, I was applying the lessons that those same people taught me, and I had the same problem. I never knew how much I was actually netting on an annual basis. I always attributed the low numbers to "write offs." It drove me crazy.

When I did take the time to calculate the net result, it was upsetting to me. The power of leverage is awesome. The power of the team is great. The power of systems is crucial. But watch out. Look at the real numbers and make sure that you aren't busting your butt to get a result that fools you to believe that you are more successful than you really are.

Outside onlookers might think you are successful. But make sure you aren't just building a larger hamster wheel. Simplify your life. Simplify, streamline, and systemize your model and figure out where the most profitable business is. *Net* more money. My suggestion is to net twice as much money as you actually need for your lifestyle.

Would that qualify as your DREAM BUSINESS scenario?

6. **Be Systematic**

I read a book back in 2002 called the *E-Myth Revisited* by Michael Gerber. It was the right timing for me, as I was beginning to ramp up my business and was feeling extremely frazzled trying to do everything myself. The one "take-away" that I got from that book was this: Work ON your business, instead of constantly working IN your business—create systems and operations so you can eventually plug people into certain positions. In addition, it is important to create a process for everything. That way, if other people come into your world, your level of service is not sacrificed.

This was a game changer for me.

Here is an example: I have worked with my wife for over a decade now. We have a great business relationship. We rarely argue. We get along great. I believe that though we are nice people, but we are far from perfect. We may get on each other's nerves sometimes but, all in all, we like each other and enjoy each other's company.

But the difference here is that by the time Nicole joined me in the real estate business, I had systems in place. She takes on certain roles and I take on certain roles. We own our roles. I never have to worry about whether or not she will do her part. Early on, she plugged into the systems. We stay out of each other's way, and we work together for a common goal. I think that is why we have been able to make it work. A lot of people can't believe how we can work together each day. We spend a lot of time together, yet we get along and respect each other in our roles for the good of our business. I believe that understanding has made all the difference.

If you want to grow your business, then people will come and go. If someone who was filling a pivotal role in your business leaves, then a big hole is left behind that needs to be filled. Do your systems take care of that? Can you plug someone in there quickly? There will be a learning curve but, if the roles are clearly defined, it won't be a steep one. If your company has accountability to its clients and effective measures in place in case of employee shake-ups, things will get done, and they'll get done well. The other advantage of creating systems is that you organize your efforts. You get to the point of dependability. You empower yourself with the ability to predict the outcomes from certain efforts and activities.

In addition to that, it is important to know what you are worth. We will tackle this in more detail further into the book but, the main point is, in order to succeed in anything, you need to continue to evolve and increase your Time Value. What is your time worth? Once you have established that, then you make decisions much more easily to bring people in to take on tasks that leverage your time.

After all, your ENERGY, MONEY, and TIME are your most valuable resources. They need to be leveraged so you can increase your value but also begin to utilize your energy, money and time doing other things in your life. If we use all of our time up working, then what is left for "living"? Understanding this balance is so important for the DREAM Business concept.

7. **You Are in Control – You Make it Look Easy.**

This sounds kind of silly. However, I do have a serious point to this. If you show up in front of your clients frazzled and stressed, and you complain about the long hours you work, and how you are just simply "maxxed out," people will not feel that they can refer business to you. They will think that you are too busy.

The truth is, they don't want to feel your negative energy. They suddenly, and maybe unconsciously, don't want to hassle you. I don't think you want that. I would hope that you want to create *more* business out of every interaction. Remember the 4X Formula.

Everyone you come into contact with is likely to notice that you are busy and productive, but they MUST feel that you can handle it, and that you can handle more. At the same time, every single client should feel that they are your only client. When you are with them, be with them. Other clients must not come into the picture during "their" time, unless there is a crucial time sensitive issue happening. Otherwise, this is "their time."

When you come across as someone who is calm and in control, that is an attractive quality. Do you agree? Remember, that is your role for them. You are the voice of calm. You are the person who relieves their stress. That is what you need to be for them. They should never see your "issues." They should never hear about your problems, about other clients who are driving you nuts. Don't talk about your crazy life, or the challenges with your daughter or son. There are a lot of single moms who work in Real Estate, and I hear them dumping on their clients about how difficult it is being a single mom and working in their Real Estate business. This is a huge mistake. Nobody wants to be an extra "problem" to someone. Your clients should never feel like a burden to you.

You must convince them that you are in total control. This is part of the process. I have turned twelve clients into licensed real estate agents. Maybe I make it look too easy! See how important this is?

8. **Turn on The Tap**

If you knew exactly how to get business, listings, or attract buyers when it was time to ramp up your business, would that give you an enormous amount of belief? A great sense of control? I refer to this surge of confidence as Turning on the Tap. Learning how to "turn on the tap" is a key element to having a DREAM Business. This whole book is dedicated to this concept. The idea of attracting business, just when you need it, is incredibly empowering.

In every market, in every city, in the middle of all the chaos, there is business to be done. People are always buying and selling homes. Tapping into that business is your goal. All of the strategies, concepts, mindsets, activities, and the tools to empower you are included in this book and, eventually, the Four Book Set and the 4X Formula Real Estate Mastery program.

Learn how to Turn on the Tap anytime you need to. That is what I want for you. Read on, if you'd like to run your own DREAM BUSINESS.

THE START – STARTING RIGHT.

THE MENTAL STATE OF SUCCESS

Now that we're getting into the teaching and training aspects of this book, I think we should take care of some housekeeping items prior to getting into the "how-to's."

I have found that people who are in the right state of mind each day tend to produce much more effectively than the average person, just purely from their own "will" to succeed. Before we go deeper, we need to take a little time and *create* that "will" to succeed.

Your ambition, confidence, and, ultimately, your success level is in direct proportion to your ability to imagine what success means to you. Are you aligned with that thought pattern? Do you need to adjust that thought pattern? I can't tell you how many times I have had to adjust my own thought patterns in my own life and, each time, I reached a new level. My mind was stretched. Once that happened, I was not able to go backwards. Even when I lost everything, I was able to build myself back up and create more wealth than I had ever experienced in a quarter of the time frame because I had created new beliefs in what I was able to accomplish. My actions were in total alignment with those new convictions and the net result was a faster route to my goals.

This will happen for you, too, if you embrace the principles in this book and take action. Obviously, I cannot make any guarantees, but I will tell you that principles I keep are exactly what I have followed to earn multiple six figures per year in the real estate business in a small town, where the price point is much lower than in the big cities and the population is under 100,000 people as of the writing of this book.

We are not taught how to succeed. We are not taught success mindsets, in our high schools. In a majority of households, we don't learn how to tap into the most effective parts of our brains in our childhoods. Please understand, this is not to criticize your parents, or your teachers, or anyone else influential in your past. They have been preparing you for a North American Lifestyle, which is to go to school and get a good education, so that you can get a good job. The safe route. However, in my opinion, the safe route carries other kinds of sacrifices with it. Because you are reading this book, I have to assume that you want more than that. You have decided to be a licensed real estate representative. You want to harness the lifestyle of the entrepreneur. You have decided to establish your own worth, your own lifestyle.

CLOSE the Back DOOR

As you make this enormous step, there will be uncertainties. There will be times of frustration. There will be times where you will doubt your ability to succeed in real estate. There will be times when you feel like you are wasting the day away as a "prisoner of hope," days when you are simply confused and fear sets in. You might even ask yourself some difficult questions:

"What the heck was I thinking?"

"Why did I decide to do this?"

"Am I worthy?"

"Why can't I seem to stir something up?"

"Why can't I find a client who is ready to buy or sell right away?"

"These successful agents just seem to have something magical about them that I don't have."

A stark conclusion enters your mind: "Man, I thought that this was going to be much easier. Maybe I am not cut out for this. Maybe I should go back to the J-O-B. Maybe I should just cut my losses. The total investment to be a real estate agent wasn't a lot of money anyway...just a few thousand."

This is what I call a "back door mentality." I'd like you to Close That Back Door! Let me clarify.

If you have a back door exit, mentally, you will not move forward and build your business with 110% commitment. The back door mentality reduces your commitment level. Because you have an escape. You have an exit. You have a "worst case scenario" in the back of your mind. If I were to put that thought pattern into actual dialogue, here is what that person would be telling themselves:

"Well, I will give this a shot. I am only financially risking just a couple thousand dollars. So, **IF IT DOESN'T WORK OUT**, then I have a fall-back...I can go back to where I was working before or find something similar."

Does this sound familiar? If you are honest with yourself, are you willing to admit that this very thought has crossed your mind? I think this defeatist thought has been in the back of every single real estate professional's mind at some point. There are a few people who have succeeded in the business that will never admit to this, but I know the unsettling feeling that most people experience, and I have tried to sum it up here succinctly. Just admit it, it's okay. But I am calling you out right now to recognize it for what it is. It is your survival instincts kicking in, that's all. Nothing more.

Let's analyze what is going on inside the brain at a moment like this:

I capitalized: **IF IT DOESN'T WORK OUT**

Do you see the problem with that statement?

If WHAT works out?

What is **IT**? This *phantom* **IT**. The real estate business? Is that the **IT**? The office you joined? Are they **IT**? Your real estate license? Is that the **IT**? The real estate market? **IT**?

There is no **IT**. The truth is...**IT** doesn't exist. You have created **IT** but **IT** has no power. No authority. No magical relevance. No influence on your success or failure whatsoever. **IT** is all in your own mind and as long as **IT** is there, you will be held back. So—what is the solution? First off, you have to realize that **IT** is not real.

IT is an excuse. It is a "reason" that will come to light when the opportunity presents itself to be the EXCUSE for your lack of success. That is all **IT** is. **IT** is outside of you. **IT** is created so that you don't have to own the blame for your failure, just in case. The fact is....**IT** does not exist. **IT** is only there if you give it some sort of power or authority in your life. Get rid of **IT**.

You must—right now—replace **IT** with the word YOU or ME. You are the **IT**. Take ownership of that. You are the person driving the bus. You are the person solely responsible for your success or failure in the real estate business. Take that responsibility and load it onto your own shoulders. **IT** will feel heavy at first but as we move through the chapters of this book, it will lighten as a newfound feeling of empowerment, and increased confidence, gives you the strength to carry that burden. That burden, responsibility, and ownership of the Phantom **IT** must be carried by you and nobody else. You cannot offload that responsibility.

You must make a decision right now, right this second. You are intent on succeeding in the real estate business and there is no other option. You are committed 100% to success. There is no back door, no side exit. There is no reason for having a "side hustle." You are not just "giving **IT** a shot." Mentally, close the back door, burn the bridge. There is no turning back. Okay? Are you with me? Let's get to it. A Different "it."

The fact that you are reading this book tells me that you are on the path to a much different **IT**. You have that range of thinking that is beyond others, and you are seeking to learn how to be successful. I don't want to diminish that. I recognize that. I applaud that. You are on your way to be in the top 20% of real estate professionals.

You are going to get the most out of this book by taking responsibility for your own success and committing to apply the steps that are taught as soon as possible. If you are a member of the online course, you will hear me say "Learn and Apply... Learn and Apply" many, many times. That is the key. This is a "work-book." By the time you reach the end, I suggest you start over and make sure that you perform the activities and then cover what you missed. I want this book to be your real estate companion. That is my hope for you.

The real learning will take place when you apply the steps and the principles that employ the elements of cognitive learning to solidify the concepts in your mind. **Reading** causes you to internalize concepts. The act of **writing**, when you handwrite concepts, ideas, or thoughts, helps build more concrete beliefs, understanding, and gives you the confidence to take action. **Acting**, taking action empowers you to overcome your habitual thought patterns, and fears. You will be empowered and you will grow as a person and a professional. Learning by doing is always the most effective way to learn. If you learn concepts more effectively by listening or watching, then you can become a member and watch the video content that works in concert with this book. I know that observation is how I personally learn more effectively and, if you are the same as me, the video will be a very good investment for you. I have even added—as a bonus for you, the reader—a special website with Tools you can use. I will refer to these Tools throughout the book and you can go and get them online anytime you want, for free. They are branded with the 4XFormula logos and will show you and your colleagues that you are utilizing the concepts in this book (and/or my course). I ask that you do not copy or reproduce these materials in any way. These Tools are copyright-protected and the logos are Trademarks of my company. You are welcome to staple your card onto the materials as handouts to your clients and I would even recommend that you use stickers. If your clients or colleagues ask you about the 4X formula logo, please explain to them that you are a 4X Agent employing the systems of the 4X formula to serve them well. This will one day be a "badge of honour" as the 4X brand becomes more recognized in time.

LET'S GET STARTED!

First, we must get your "Why" clarified. Next, we will help you set your goals to help you reach your ultimate destination, and then we will determine the qualities you'll need to be a successful 4X Agent. Throughout the rest of the book, I will refer to these winning traits as they apply to certain parts of our activities, habits, and mindsets.

In order to ensure career longevity, to give you that grit to keep going, and to help you close the back door and look forward, it is important to establish WHAT you want to achieve and WHY you want to achieve that.

We have to talk about the Why. "*Why? Because...THAT'S why*!" is what my mom used to say to me. I used to always ask Why. It drove her crazy but I needed to understand. After a while, I stopped asking Why and then just accepted things as they were presented to me. Then I got older and became an adult; I began to distill the information coming at me. I started to meet successful people. I began to question the self-limiting beliefs that were holding me back. I am still battling those "thoughts in my head" every day. I came from very humble beginnings. I had no idea what success was... or if I even deserved it.

My first "Why", was simply this: I never want to have to fight with my wife about money issues. That was it. I eventually started to go deeper. I began to ask Why again, and more often. There are so many times in our lives, and in our careers, when we forget to ask this question. But before we get too deep into applying WHY into our *outer* social lives, I want you to focus right now on your INNER WHY. The deep WHY. The heart of the WHY. Once I learned to do this...it changed my life.

WHY are you a Real Estate Agent?

Why did you order up the Real Estate Course and put yourself through those gruelling lessons?

Why do you feel that you can succeed at real estate?

Why should your spouse or life partner or family support you?

Why are you reading this book right now?

Why do you want to become better?

Why do you want to earn $____ dollars this year?

WHY? There are many ways to answer these questions. I am asking you to think deeply about them. Ask the question. Answer it. Think about that answer and then follow it to a deeper WHY. Keep doing it....by the sixth or seventh time, you will get to the heart of the reason...the REAL WHY. The INNER Why.

Here is an example:

Q. ***Why did you make a decision to become a licensed real estate agent?***

A. Because I saw how much my friend Darren was making and I thought I could do better than him.

Q. ***Why did that knowledge about Darren turn you on to real estate?***

A. Because I am working in a job at ____________ and I don't see me doing this the rest of my life.

Q. ***Why did you want to leave your job so badly?***

A. Because I didn't like how I was treated, and I didn't think my income would increase if I stayed there. Plus Darren makes pretty good money.

Q. ***Why is it important for you to earn more money than your last job?***

A. Because I want to stop constantly struggling and I want to know that if I put out more effort, I can potentially earn more money.

Q. ***Why is earning more money important to you?***

A. So I can save money, make investments, put money away for my kids' education, drive a nicer car, and have a nicer house.

Q. ***Why is it so important to have all of those things that money can get you?***

A. Well, I grew up in a family that struggled financially. My parents fought about money all the time. They were always stressed out and unable to help me out financially when I needed it. I don't want to live my life like that. I want to be able to give my kids a chance to have a better life than I did.. I was unhappy at my job and felt unfulfilled there. I felt helpless.

Okay....so you see where we ended up. It all started with me comparing myself to Darren, the friend who seemed to be making pretty good money, to eventually uncovering the heart of the matter, the real motivation: I wanted to empower myself and my family. That motivation is much more powerful than simply making more money. Money is part of it. What can the money do for you? What will that money provide? How will that money change your life? What will change? How will you feel about that? What will bring you true fulfilment? When you see your kids graduate, knowing that you have the resources to help them go on to higher learning, how will that make you feel? What about having the resources to help them make their first real estate vestment? That fires me up!

This is what will get you out of bed every morning.

How does that sound? The beautiful thing about empowerment is that it is fueled by burning desire. There is emotion attached to this empowerment, and it drives you. Empowerment is the gasoline. Real estate is the right vehicle. It is the fastest vehicle. But it won't move if there is no gasoline in the vehicle. The clearly defined "Why" is the gasoline for the vehicle.

In the Tools section at 4Xformula.com/attractbook, go and get the Why Worksheet tool and download that. Do not move on in this book until you have taken the time to fill out that worksheet. You will literally feel the adrenaline start pumping in your veins as self-belief begins to build inside you, as the synapses in your brain begin to adopt this new belief. This exercise will help you build a picture in your mind: Your brain will see the result and then all of your inner resources will begin working together to help you realize that new vision. This is how you empower yourself. I can't do it for you, but I can lead in the right direction and give you the Tools.

Napoleon Hill wrote a quote in his book "Think and Grow Rich" that's says:

"Whatever the mind of man can first conceive, and BELIEVE, he will achieve."

The act of thinking deeply about your specific "WHY" and doing the exercise is the "conception. This is where you allow your mind to conceive of the lifestyle that you want. The worksheet helps you create a strong visualization of that, and then, as you begin to picture that lifestyle in your own mind, you are literally creating a new belief. The fact is your mind is already full of many different types of beliefs that have been solidified in your mind. Some of these beliefs will serve you well. Some of these beliefs will hold you back. In order to "close the back door" and move forward with confidence, it is important for you to believe in yourself. You must create clarity. Just simply "making enough money" to replace a J-O-B is not powerful enough to take you to the next level. When times get tough, or you need to stretch yourself in some way to learn and apply, you will do it, if you have created a strong WHY to drive you through those bumpy roads. Belief is the key to Achieving what you want.

Here is my quote that is connected to Napoleon Hill's quote:

"If you do not BELIEVE, you will NOT ACHIEVE."

It's as simple as that. You may have some "limiting beliefs" already built in to your subconscious, that you need to replace. You may have certain beliefs that have you thinking that you don't deserve a nice lifestyle, for whatever reason. You may be confused right now. You may be so caught up in "survival mode" mentality, that you can't even visualize what it would be like. That is why this exercise is so important. All of the other strategies that I teach to help you succeed in Real Estate will mean nothing until you know WHY you are doing it. CLARIFY the Why and you will have the gas in the tank to take you where you want to go. Everything we do from here on out, is to take that newfound "seed of belief" and help it grow and grow until you achieve what you want. Then once you achieve that, you will begin to build new beliefs and so on. Get excited!

You have to take action. If you don't, you are short-changing yourself. 90% of all real estate agents out there have never taken the time to do this, including the so-called successful agents, who are out there, chasing money. Believe it or not, you can make over $500,000 in GCI (Gross Commissionable Income, the broker's take from a sale before they pay you) and still be in "Survival Mode" if you have no idea WHY you are working so hard. I was that person once, and I paid a big price for it. Once I began to understand my WHY, my life changed and, to be perfectly honest, the business actually got easier.

If I were to sum it up…I'm trying to get you out of "Survival Mode" and into "Thrive Mode." Thrive Mode means making more money than you need to pay bills and take care of the basic household needs. Putting money away for future investments. Accumulating assets. Saving money for future retirement, and for your kids' future. Moving up from "just covering the bills" and being constantly in debt, to enjoying life and never stressing about paying the bills. There is a certain confidence and peace of mind that sets in, when you have consistent income and a minimum of $100,000 in the bank. Once you reach that level, you move into Thrive Mode and the world opens up to you. It gets easier to win listings, and to lock in new buyers and leads. Everything just gets easier.

So, let's get you there. Go and download the worksheet and complete the exercise. Talk it over with your spouse or trusted loved one or friend. Share your dreams and desires and goals for your life. Open up your mind and allow yourself to imagine a better life and then commit to achieving it. That better life is going to be your Destination…your first destination…

GOAL SETTING FOR REAL ESTATE

Now that you have done the work to establish **What** you want, and **Why** you want it, ...we must map out the destination and help you get there. You have taken the time, on the **Why Worksheet**, to establish your current reality, your starting point. The Destination is solidified and now it is about the journey. In all journeys, there are little benchmarks or road signs, indicators that you are either on track... or off track. It has happened to me many times when I'm using my navigation app on my phone or vehicle. If I miss a turn and drive right by, the app tells me to make a legal U-turn, when possible, or it will re-calculate the route for me and begin giving me new instructions.

Corrections *will* have to be made as you move towards your destination or goal. Sometimes we miss the goal (or one of our "mini-goals") and that is okay, as long as you keep on moving. You simply need to find a different route to get there. The key is to stay in motion. The Goal will drive you. Keep your eye on the Goal. Don't turn off the navigation.

Have you ever been driving along the road, listening to a podcast or an awesome playlist in your vehicle and the darn navigation keeps piping up and reminding you of when the next turn is? That can be quite aggravating. I sometimes find myself yelling at the navigation system... *"I get it...I need to take a slight turn in 1 kilometer or in 300 meters...enough already...stop interrupting this podcast!! Sheesh..."*

When we set goals, we need to be our own (sometimes aggravating) navigation system. We need to be constantly reminding ourselves of the next destination. We must be fully conscious of the end goal and constantly interrupt our "auto-pilot" minds to stay focussed on our defined route.

Building anticipation is the key. There is a powerful adjustment in our thought patterns that occurs when we move from wishing and hoping to anticipation. Anticipation denotes a certain level of commitment, doesn't it? That's what you want. Stop wishing and hoping. Anticipate.

There are three basic levels of anticipation:

1. Positive Anticipation: You are fired up and excited and just can't wait to get there.
2. Luke-Warm Anticipation: You are going to the gas station to get gas. Ho-hum.
3. Negative Anticipation: You are a prisoner on death row; this is the worst-case scenario.

All three levels of anticipation have different results but carry with them the same level of belief.

I remember, when I was eight years old, my mother took my brother and me on a bus trip from our little town—an hour outside of Vancouver, British Columbia—to Disneyland in California. Yes, a bus trip. It was much cheaper, then, to take a bus than flying there on an airplane. We were on the road for four days to get to Disneyland, but our excitement never wavered. We knew where we were going, and we knew it was going to be awesome once we got there. In those days, people could smoke cigarettes on the bus. This was the Seventies and the busses were not quite as comfortable as they are today. There were no built-in televisions or music playing. We had to figure out different ways to entertain ourselves.

It was a gruelling four days of travel on that smoky bus, but we were excited. We knew where we were going. We had a big paper map and mom showed us where we were every place we stopped, and we could see that we were getting closer to the goal. As we neared, the positive anticipation grew and grew; we were gushing with excitement to get to that magical land of Disney!

At Disneyland, we had the time of our lives. We had never seen a place like it before. It was amazing, everything we dreamed it would be and more. We were on a three-day high. Then, on the fourth day, it was time to don our Mickey Mouse ears, load onto the bus and make our way back home. This level of anticipation was a lot different from the one we'd had before, on the way down. This one was a four-day bus ride, leaving the magical land of Disney and going back to the farm in our little town. Back to regular life, where we had to get up early, pick eggs do our chores, and then go to school every day. The magic was over. Now we were on our way back, away from the "awesomeness" of Disneyland, on this hot, sticky, bouncy, uncomfortable, smoky bus full of aggravating people. It seemed incredibly bumpy now. Everything seemed to be annoying me on the way back. I knew the destination we were headed to. It was not an exciting destination. It was a major "downer." What a difference from the ride down from Vancouver, when nothing had seemed to bother me, when I was so excited that I didn't even notice all the aggravating aspects of travel. My eye was on the goal. I was bubbling inside. I was picturing and imagining the fun I was going to have. I was experiencing the excitement before even getting there. I was filled with positive anticipation and all the negative things about riding in an uncomfortable, smoke-filled bus packed with a bunch of people were non-existent on the way there. I can still remember how I felt, and that was 43 years ago. My mind was filled with positive thoughts, focussed on the bigger picture: The Magical World of Disneyland, the happiest place on earth. That was it.

But now that we were driving back home, I felt this sinking feeling. I understood that the Disneyland magic couldn't last forever. I knew that I had to go back home at some point but that bus ride was a version of "hell" to me. It was horrible.

Do you see how important it is to do the work on the "Why"? Really go deep in that. Imagine the life you will have. Close your eyes and think about it. Create many vivid pictures in your mind. Get excited about it. Create the Positive Anticipation, with emotion mixed in, and you will be unstoppable.

Here is another simpler illustration:

Have you ever gone to a restaurant that you have never been to, and looked at the menu, and found it difficult to decide what to order? Then, compare that feeling to when you visited a restaurant you had been to before and had a fantastic experience. You loved this certain dish, and you were totally confident that you wanted that tantalizing, flavourful, menu item again, so you didn't even need to look at the menu. Your GOAL was to go to that specific restaurant to order that specific dish? Your Goal was defined and clear. Right? You know that feeling of positive anticipation. You actually salivate a little thinking about that awesome dish. You are excited. Your body is simply reacting to what you are imagining. That is how powerful your mind is, and also how powerful Goal Setting can be for you.

You need to know that the top 20% real estate earners are "Goal Setters" or even better, "Goal Getters." They know what they want. They know Why they want it. They have positive expectation built into their minds and will accept nothing less but to achieve that Goal or "set of goals." Being

Goal Getters, they anticipate to see what they want in their minds before they actually achieve it.

This exercise is just as important as learning a script to figure out how to deal with a "sign call." I would contest that you will get more results in your life from these exercises, even if you never learned another thing. Showing up with *100% commitment*, and then building on that concrete belief is the key.

Determine the Destination!

Know the "life" you want to create. Get clarity on the starting point you are coming from. Determine what your financial needs are to "survive" this year, and then create your vision for "Thrive." Get on the Bus, Determine the Destination, and get to California. Then think deeply and clarify your Why. What is your "Thriving Lifestyle"? What is your Disneyland?

To be clear, Goal Setting for Real Estate is all about money. I suggest you also take some time to think about the other areas of your life: your spiritual goals, your family goals, your health goals, and your learning goals. All of these goals are vitally important to live a well-rounded life of fulfillment and happiness. I am a major advocate of achieving a balanced life. Money is not the solution to everything. I do not mean to steer anyone away from that balance by focussing solely on money. However, for the purposes of this subject matter, I am going to be narrowing in on Commission Cheques and money. I am going to assume that you want more financial reward, not less.

First Step: Find out what the average **GCI** (Gross Commission Income) **per DEAL** or transaction is in your office right now. Ask your Broker/Owner/Team Leader what the average commission was on the total amount of transactions conveyed in your office for your own marketplace. This is an important step in your goal setting. This number is your GCI, before splits, or office fees. I call it the "Dollar per Deal" number. Every year I look at all my commissions and I divide them out by the number of transactions that closed and paid out, and I quickly learn what my average "Dollar per Deal" is. Knowing this number helps me set new goals for the next year.

So, if I want to earn $350,000 next year in Gross Commissions and my average "Dollar per Deal" is $6,345 per deal, then it's just easy math: 350,000 divided by 6345 = 55.16. So, I know I have to do 55 deals if I want to earn $350,000 in GCI. 55 deals divided by 12 months = 4.6 deals per month. So, in this case, I would set my goal for **five deals every month**. 5 x 6,345 = $31,725/m. Now, in my head, on my goal sheets, on my board, I focus on those five deals per month and, adding up my commission payouts, I am shooting for a minimum of $30,000 per month.

At this point, the following two questions pop up:

1. How many listings do I need in order to do five deals per month?
2. How many buyers do I need to work with in order to do five deals per month?

Each transaction has a different timeline. Each buyer has a different date on their purchase contract. You can't control when a buyer buys, nor the finishing date by which the buyer is contractually bound to buy your listing. I have had some buyers on my list for two years. I have had listing clients on my list for a year before they eventually go on the market. Alternatively, I have people call me up and we are on the market in three days and it sells in a week. Or, I "lock in" a buyer, we go to work, and they complete in 15 days, adding to the deal flow of that same month! That was totally unexpected. These are all moving targets. Consistency is the key. Remember when I introduced you to the idea of planting the seed? *Seed planting* is in your control. You will hear me say, "You can't pull on a blade of grass, and make it grow faster, but you can plant the seeds and watch the plant grow. You control the planting of seeds. Plant many, many seeds every day." Do this, and growth will happen even when you don't expect it, filling up your timelines. Think of your business this way. Constantly seed planting.

Constantly...consistently...always.

"*The 3 Ls*" & The 10 and 2 Rule

So, we need to set the goals for the Gross Commission, the number of deals it takes to get there, and how many listings we will need to achieve that many deals. First things first, we need "*The 3 Ls.*"

LEADS. LEADS. LEADS. At this stage of your business building, this is what "*The 3 Ls*" represent. Later, in your business building "*The 3 Ls*" will represent LEADS, LISTINGS and LEVERAGE. But right now, you are focussed on LEADS. That's it.

If your WHY is set up and your vision of your future is solidified, and you have taken the time to produce a proper Goal Setting plan, then you know the END RESULT you want. You will add your Dollar per Deals up every month and, at the end of the year, you will do some more math and see if you either came close, or met, or exceeded your financial goals. The WHY is the fuel for the Vehicle.

If WHY is your fuel, then your LEADS are the engine that runs the vehicle. If you have no leads, a small amount of leads or if you are "hatching leads" (sitting on a lead trying to hatch it like a hen instead of getting more leads) then it's like having a Lamborghini with an engine from a 1997 Chevy Sprint under the hood. LEADS are the LEAD Measure to get you to the LAG Measure, which is the sales number figure you find at the end of the month or the year. It's easy to measure. Just add it up.

What does it take to get you to that LAG measure? It takes the ability to consistently and constantly attract LEADS and put them into your pipeline, every single day.

It is my position that all you need is one to three leads day to make $350,000 per year. For this example, 2 le per day is your LEAD MEASURE.

Right now, I can actually picture your eyebrows raising or furrowing! Relax your face and smile. Take the pressure off yourself. You don't need 100 to 200 leads per month, like those Zillow or Trulia or "Lead Generator" companies are telling you. You don't. You simply need to apply the steps that we teach further on in this book and, ultimately, in the 4X Formula Quick Commission Accelerator Course. This has been my practice for over 23 years, and it has never failed me. I have never "cold called" or "door-knocked" (without an honest purpose) and I have never paid for leads.

The way the math works, I call the **10 and 2 Rule**. Here's how it goes: Let's say you average two LEADS per day. Over a 30-day period, you will have recorded 60 Leads into your Tracker. Go get your LEAD Tracker at 4XFormula.com/attractbook. Based on the 10 and 2 Rule, that will give you two *Active Clients* for every 10 that go on the list. That leaves you with 12 Active Clients. You may experience different ratios but, in my experience, it is about 50/50 buyers and sellers, six buyers and six sellers. Usually, 50% of the buyers you attract will need to sell something. Now, are they all going to close a transaction in the next 30 days? Probably not. That's why consistency is the key; you always have some people moving into the pipeline and others moving into the processing part of the transaction. A certain percentage of these people will move into the NOW Category while you are still nurturing the SOON and FUTURE category people and—as you do more deals, and your time in the business accumulates—you will need to pay attention to the PAST business. This is how you leverage your efforts. This is where the other **3 Ls** come into play. It will get easier to get LEADS as you progress in your business.

The other leverage point is the **4X Formula**. Every listing creates four commission cheques. Remember? Listings attract buyers. Never forget that. Ever. Listings are the key to more business. *If you have far more listings than you can handle, you attract less business. In some cases, you even repel business. There is a sweet spot to achieve, so that you have the most efficient business garnering the best leads for your business.* Maybe go back and read those last three sentences again. This is really, important to understand.

If every listing creates four deals, then how many listings do you need to create an opportunity to earn $350,000? Remember our average GCI is $6,345 x 4 = $25,380. Let's take $350,000 divided by $25,380 = 13.79 listings. Let's round up to 14. Now, some listings don't sell. Other listings sell too quickly to attract a buyer. Some people who list homes are not buying again. One example of that is a client who owns a rental investment property. They already have their family home and may not be buying again. Sometimes, they'll sell that investment and buy two other investments. You just never know. To allow for these inconsistencies, I would make the goal of listing five properties per month. Even if you fall short and only list an average of *three* properties per month, you may still hit the number of deals necessary to make $350,000 if you become a master at attracting buyers off of those listings. There are a lot of different ways to reach the goal.

I remember when I thought that I needed to carry 25 to 30 listings all the time in order to make that much money. I was horrendously wrong. With the focus of the 4X Formula, you can run your business easily, with little stress, no paid staff and a lot of profit. However, once you get to this point, you can afford to have a paid administrator to take care of the little details. This will be someone who is excellent at what I refer to as "Listing Maintenance" organizing your lead capture, nurturing your past clients, and taking care of paperwork so that you can have more time and control over your life. This is another form of **leverage**. This is where balance kicks in, and when your WHY Worksheet items begin to be realized.

What happens now? Belief sets in and begins to solidify. There is no turning back. Go ahead... imagine this in your mind for a minute. See it happening. Picture yourself communicating with your Administration Assistant. Allow yourself to experience that feeling of accomplishment. This is a business now, a very profitable business. You are running a business that is a going concern and a growing concern.

So now, go and get your Goal Setting Worksheets and work through those tools.

How many LEADS per year? How many listings per year? How many deals per year? Then break those numbers down to a monthly goal for all of those metrics. Download the Annual Goal Tracker and enter your data on a monthly basis, adding up each month and keeping a running total to hit your year-end target. Do the worksheet. Fill out the Goal Setting Worksheet. This is a form I created so that you can cut it out and put in a nice frame (or an ugly frame, it's up to you.) I would frame at least three of these and have them everywhere. You could even hang one in the bathroom on the wall, or on the counter so you see it when you are brushing your teeth every morning. Another one could be by your desk where you work so that you see it all the time. Or maybe by your bed so that you see it first thing in the morning and when you go to bed at night.

You are jogging your mind constantly, keeping yourself on track. Building belief. Putting **IT** on your shoulders. This is very important. Then download the LEAD TRACKER and keep that with you, or on your desk, or on your fridge with a magnet. Write two LEADS per day on your form. This is the **no-excuse form**, and it needs two new names to go on it, every single day. Every day. Without exception. If you take Sundays off as a family day, that is okay. Calculate and Goal Set accordingly.

Now your mind is focussed, laser focussed. It's easy to focus on easy things. Easy concepts. At least, that is how *my* mind works. If I want to achieve $350,000 per year, what do I need to do every day? Two leads per day. Okay, I can do that. I can focus on that. Two leads per day. Two meaningful discussions about real estate every day with two different people; each of those people go on the Lead Tracker form. It cannot be any simpler. Two LEADS per DAY. That is your rally cry now. Write that on your mirror in lipstick. On your computer screensaver when it boots up...bam.... Two LEADS per DAY! Your calendar on your phone should have it down as an All-Day event....Two LEADS per DAY. Or put it at the end of your day at 9:30pm: Two Leads today? With a question mark. Find ways to keep your brain totally focussed on Two LEADS per day. Now, your Goals may be different, so whatever that figure is for you, based on your own calculations, is *the number*. It may be Three LEADS per day or one per day. It's up to you.

This is the game. You want to win the day every day, win the day by getting Two LEADS per Day! It's a game now. But it's not a proper game unless you keep score. That is why we have the trackers. Keeping score increases the intensity. You are only competing with yourself to achieve your goals. Don't worry about anyone else. This is your game, and you will achieve it. You know the end result you want. You know the end of the month goal that you want. You know the goal that you want to achieve at the end of the year! But the metric, the measuring stick, the road sign that lets you know you are on your way there, is your LEADS per DAY metric. At the end of the month, did you write down 50 to 60 names? That is what you are shooting for. Then highlight the names of the people who are now working with you and have become a "Contact Card" or even a "File" or "Listing or Buying Contact." How many? When you highlight those names, are there 10 to 12 names highlighted? That is now your conversion rate. Remember the **10 and 2 Rule**? That is why it is so important to record everything so you can begin to understand your conversion rate. You should shoot for 20%. Once those two people per day become referrals, and once past business is coming back to you on a regular basis, you will see your conversion rates increase substantially. This is when the business gets easier. Excited? I am. I hope you are. Get excited! Emotion is a powerful driver to get you to where you want to go. Wake up each day excited. When you add a new name to your Tracker, get excited. When you add *another* new name to your tracker...get excited, about that, too. When you see that message pop up, *Two LEADS today*? you can say – "oh, yeah!!! Yes, I did." *There* is that little hit of dopamine for you. We all love it. We all crave it. That's why those games on your phone are so addicting; it's the cycle of effort, reward...effort, reward. The dopamine hit that we feel. Well, just apply that to your business. "Game-ify" your business!

Increase your conversion rates, increase your dollar per hour. One of my favorite activities, every winter when I am planning the next year, is when I add everything up. I calculate my conversion rates, my average monthly GCI, my average Deal Per Month for the year, my average Dollar per Deal. Then I have all of the material needed to set my goals for the new year. However, there is one more calculation that I need to perform: My Dollars per Hour.

What is your time worth? That is what it boils down to. Once you know what your time is actually worth, you begin to make better decisions on where you spend your time. If you want to increase your $/hr you need to find the top 20% of the activities that get you 80% of the money that you earn. As you build your business, it's important to know this number and figure out how to increase it every year. When you have a client who is wasting your time, it is easier to let them go, refer them to someone else, or have a tougher conversation with them, when you are certain of the value of your time. When you are tempted to scroll a little longer on

Instagram or Facebook or get caught up in the TikTok vortex, it is easier to pull yourself away, when you know what your time is worth. Here is a simple example of a calculation: 350,000 divided by (48x50=2400) = Dollar per Hour

If you work 48 weeks per year and estimate that you work 50 hours per week then your time is worth $146 per hour. If you can earn the same amount of money, but only work 42 weeks per year, then your time is worth $166 per hour. Talk about paid vacation time. Right? The key is to make those 50 hours count. Don't waste those working hours. Become intensely focussed and your $/hr will increase substantially. When you get better at converting leads and winning listing meetings, then your $/hr will increase. When you begin to get an abundance of referrals coming to you from past clientele, your $/hr will increase. You should always know your $/hr so you make proper decisions with your time. Time is non-refundable. Once it is spent, it is gone. Ask yourself: *What is the value of my time when I am maximizing it, and when I am wasting it*?

Another example of this exercise is when you pay someone $20 per hour to mow your lawn because you are working six and seven days per week. That can be a very easy decision to make. Now, while that person is mowing your lawn, you may be spending your time with your loved ones or enjoying a game of golf, or shopping with your friends. That is okay. These are your non-working hours. These hours don't count. If you decide to mow the lawn, (and by the way, it's okay to mow your lawn; some people *love* mowing their lawn) then you are effectively paying $145/hour to mow your lawn—that's how much your time is worth. This is not a good investment of your time. Plus, that person you hire to mow your lawn will most likely do a better job than you can.

Know your $/hr and you begin to think like a businessperson, and you utilize the power of multiplication and the power of leverage.

THE 9 FACETS OF THE 4X AGENT

As you move through this book and implement the systems and tools that I give to you, something will happen. You will change. You will transform. New habits will now dominate your life. New thought patterns and ideals and beliefs will begin to seep into your subconscious, and you will begin to set new standards for yourself. This is my hope for you. Who YOU become...as you succeed in your business, will be the greatest reward you find from reading this book. It's about more than just money.

The next section is devoted to the 4X Agent. This is the identity that I am hoping everyone who reads this book will eventually adopt. We are ambassadors of the brand and of our industry. If it applies to you, the name REALTOR® carries with it a certain meaning. That meaning is different for a lot of people. What are the characteristics of a person carrying that brand?

You can find a simple definition of "REALTOR®" on the CREA or NAR websites. But I would say that this definition covers the minimum standard. This definition now allows people to call themselves REALTORs® with absolutely no obligation expected.

Is that what a REALTOR® is? Isn't the MLS system composed and created with the ideals of the "Rules of Cooperation"? Is offering no Agency to the Seller, then offering $1.00 to a cooperating agent why the system was created? I am not going to get into the politics or go "toe-to-toe" with the Competition Act right now in this book, but I am asking the question so that we establish a clear foundation of operation. I am not striving for the minimum standards. I am not attacking someone else's business plan. I am simply establishing that this book is dedicated to someone who wants to embody the standard to which the titles *REALTOR®*, *4X Agent, Real Estate Professional*, *Real Estate Broker, Real Estate Agent* and *Real Estate Representative* should be held. What about the brand you represent ? You are representing your company as a licensed Real Estate Agent. You are an ambassador of that brand. The same goes for people who take my course and read this book. Once you begin to implement the strategies, tactics and systems of the 4X Agent, you become an ambassador of the brand, and—ultimately—of the real estate Industry as a whole, in North America and beyond.

The Nine Facets of the 4X Agent embody what a real estate professional serving the public is meant to be. If you make it your goal to embody these facets , you will enjoy success. It is a mindset. It is a culture. If you have listened to my podcast, you will have heard me talk about these Nine Facets. (On any podcast platform, look for 4X Formula Real Estate.)

THE 9 FACETS TO BECOMING A COMPLETE 4X AGENT

Here are the Nine Facets we need to integrate in order to be a complete 4X Agent and to experience the DREAM Real Estate business:

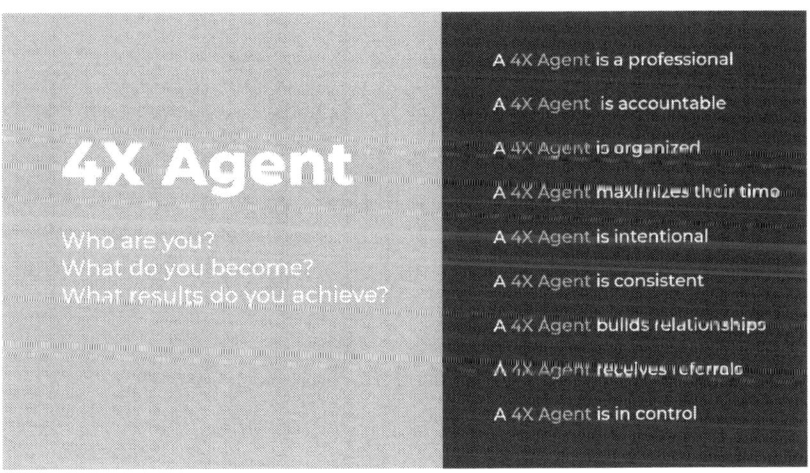

1. A 4X Agent is a **Professional**

A professional is in a constant state of mastering their craft. A professional is consumed with all aspects of their profession. A professional is in a never-ending search of betterment. A professional is constantly learning and constantly applying what they learn. A professional will voluntarily hold themselves to a higher standard. Professionals conduct themselves appropriately in public and continue to be a positive ambassador of their profession.

2. A 4X Agent is **Accountable**

Accountability is the cornerstone of trust. An accountable person is one who others can "count on." It's a simple concept but, sometimes, it is hard to achieve. Your word is your bond, no matter how difficult it is to keep that word. There are many agents out there who are very accountable by nature, but they are not accountable to themselves. This is the one aspect of accountability that a lot of people struggle with. I implore you to commit to absolute accountability in all aspects of your life to others and to yourself, equally. When you commit in writing to your goals and continuously asking yourself WHY, you hold yourself accountable to that commitment.

3. A 4X Agent is **Organized**

Organization is a critical aspect of success. I don't hear a lot of trainers or coaches talk about this, but they should. Keep yourself organized. Keep your team organized. Keep your day organized. Utilize tools to help you. Employ people if you must. I created systems for you for a definite reason. When you are organized your time becomes more valuable. When clients see that you have a system, and you pay attention to the details, they become relaxed and the bond of trust strengthens. Being organized allows you to achieve all the other aspects of a 4X Agent, much more easily. Organize, your morning, your day, your weeks and your life and watch what happens.

4. A 4X Agent **Maximizes their Time**

We have already touched on this earlier but look at how it all fits together: Being on time supports our Accountability facet, and being organized maximizes our time better. Time is a precious commodity. Time is non-refundable. Calculating your "time value" is so important; it helps you quantify, and qualify, where and how you spend your time. Attack each day with a sense of urgency, to maximize the output of that day. When you make a schedule, and commit to that schedule, and work by appointment, you will maximize your time and your "dollar per hour" will increase.

5. A 4X Agent is **Intentional**

Intention. I remember in my "acting days", my acting coach would ask me, "What is your intention in this scene?." When you know your intention, then you know HOW to say the lines...you don't have to "act." When you operate your real estate business with intention, you know the result you are trying to accomplish, each day, each week, and each month, to get the desired result for the year. When you are scheduling your days or weeks, or meeting someone for the first time, or marketing a listing, there is always a clearly defined intention. When you are signing documents for a listing, there is a certain systematic approach to that. When you set up an open house event, there are intentional steps to take to create a successful outcome. Everything you do is Intentional. Define your Intentions with each action that you take, and the results will speak for themselves.

6. A 4X Agent is **Consistent**

Consistency is powerful. If you are operating with the appropriate intention, then the results will come. Trust in the process. Get up and work every day. Be consistent with your attitude, and your actions. Be accountable to what you commit to doing. There is never one thing that brings you success. It is a combination of many different little actions done consistently that will build success into your life. In order to design a real estate business where you get paid every single month, you need to build consistency into your business so that the pipeline of activity is constant. It will not happen overnight, but it will happen, if you employ the strategies taught in this book, consistently.

7. A 4X Agent **Builds Relationships**

You are in the business of creating and maintaining relationships with many people. That is **it**, in a nutshell. The more relationships you create and maintain, the more successful you will be. If you conduct yourself as a professional—and operate with accountability, intention and consistency—over time, you will build some very important and profitable relationships. The bonus is that, in the process, you will make a lot of friends. That is never a bad thing. There are varying degrees of relationships that you will discover as time progresses. Each type of relationship that you encounter, and nurture, will become a planted seed that will germinate and produce fruit in ways that you cannot foresee. Focus on the planting and nurturing, intentionally, every day, and you will experience success. Every relationship is a new plant that will produce fruit, if nurtured properly.

8. A 4X Agent **Receives Referrals**

When you employ, implement, and personify the above seven facets, you will BECOME a person who simply Receives Referrals. It is who you are. It is in your DNA. You ARE a person who Receives Referrals. Full Stop. In fact, you will not be able to stop it. Every week, you will get a phone call or an email or a Facebook Messenger message or a DM on Instagram or whatever new forms of contact might arise, asking you to contact somebody to talk about real estate. People will refer business to you because you deserve it, not because you are entitled to it. They will become your billboards and do your marketing for you—for FREE! But, in doing so, you will have to become skilled at creating relationships with other professionals to formulate strategic alliances and other reciprocal referral sources. Build an army of Referral Sources and you will never be looking for business.

9. A 4X Agent is **In Control**

Imagine integrating all of these facets into your business, and then having no sense of control. I don't think it is possible. This is the ultimate goal. To have control. This crazy real estate business has so many moving parts and, of course, there are many things that are simply out of our control. But we *can* control specific parts of our lives and our business.

You drive the bus. You choose who gets on the bus. You decide on how fast the bus goes and where the destination is going to be. You decide on the mini-destinations that will get you to the ultimate destination and you create the positive atmosphere for everyone that is on the bus with you. You are in control of it all. You may hit some bumps along the way. You may have to take a few detours, maybe get a flat tire. Sometimes, you will feel like you are running out of gas. You will have to fuel up sometimes. Go back to the Why worksheet and go over your Goal worksheet and fill up that tank. Watch a Video, or listen to a podcast and shift gears, and get back on track. Read one of the chapters in this book. Become a member of the 4X formula community. Everything that I have designed is to keep you on track to the goals that you set out for yourself. You may take some side trips. That's okay. We are all human. But never forget that you are in control of everything that you can control.

I hope you agree with me, that you are fully capable of fulfilling these Nine Facets. There is nothing special about any one of these facets but, when you combine all nine together, you possess the attributes of all the most successful real estate agents.

THE 4X AGENT'S 12 POINTS OF POWER

What attributes over and above the Nine Facets does a successful real estate professional need to possess attain true success? The 12 points of power below are self-explanatory. Read them out loud every day along with your goals and your Why worksheet; you'll begin to transform your thinking and your habitual behaviours and become an unstoppable real estate marketing machine. As we move through the lessons in the following chapters, you will see how everything is all interwoven to create a persona, an ideal, a culture, and an identity, all of which will ensure a successful and fulfilling, real estate lifestyle for you and your family or loved ones.

It is my hope that there will, one day, be an army of 4X Agents operating in North American and all over the world, employing the Nine Facets, and adopting the 12 Points of Power into their lives. The general public and other real estate agents will see a subtle or, maybe, a not-so-subtle difference, in how the 4X Agent commands their lives. Begin now to hold yourself to a higher standard. The new 4X Agent Standard:

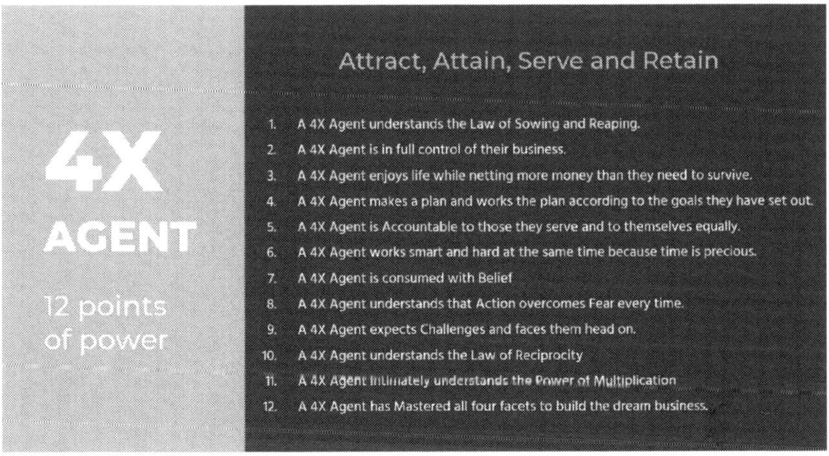

A 4X Agent has mastered all four Pillars to build the Dream Business.

FOUR MINDSHIFTS FOR NEW REAL ESTATE AGENTS

Full Throttle

I understand and agree that it is important to have 'work-life balance'. BUT—and there is a huge BUT here—I want you to understand that you can't simply decide to have 'work-life balance' unless you have decided that you are okay with living in a tent somewhere. That may be one option as a lifestyle choice but, the truth is, you have to be out of balance, first, in order to achieve balance. As paradoxical as that seems, it's the truth. There is a "weight" that must be achieved first, and that weight is your concentrated effort. Balance doesn't just happen.

Picture a scale: One end of the scale is already weighted down. To create balance, there also needs to be weight on the other side. A dream, a wish or an ideal, is not going to bring the scale into balance. Something needs to be loaded on, in order to even the scales. And that "something" would be your EMT (Energy, Money and Time).

This is where the Full Throttle part comes in. I call it the LIFT OFF.

Let's talk about LIFT OFF in terms of what is required for an airplane to get off the ground. When an airplane pilot is getting ready for take-off, he makes sure he goes over his whole checklist to ensure that everything is in order. He waits to get clearance from the control tower and then heads to the runway. Once he gets the go-ahead, he then pushes the throttle forward, accelerating the engines. The plane begins to pick up speed and starts moving very fast. The pilot pushes the throttle right to the maximum speed. All the way. Once he hits that crucial speed, the rest of the machine begins to respond, and the plane starts to take flight. LIFT OFF. Now, here's the thing — if the pilot lets off the throttle even a little bit, the plane will fail to lift off the ground, and won't launch into the air. The pilot must keep that throttle all the way down in order to experience lift off. He is not guessing which speed he needs to be at, to experience lift off. He knows that there is no negotiation there; lift off simply will not happen unless he is going at the maximum speed. This is where the "balance" comes in. Shortly after lift off, as the plane gains altitude and he levels the plane out at 30,000 feet or so, he actually has to ease off the throttle, or the engines will burn out. The plane will be damaged if he keeps the throttle at full blast. At that altitude the air is thinner and there is less friction, so the plane actually gets to the destination a lot quicker, with much less effort, so the engines do not need to work as hard.

This is where I'm going with my balance of life metaphor. In the beginning, your focus has to be entirely on activities, effort, and focus that gets you into momentum, at top speed, to get you to lift off. Little spurts don't work.

A lot of people think they are running a 40-yard dash instead of a 100-yard dash. They slow down for bit, and then when they aren't experiencing lift off, they amp it up again. By doing this, they just keep killing the momentum. This keeps them in a zone of survival and they never get out to experience The Thrive zone. What can happen is that some people stay in this cycle, and others potentially reach burnout. They never seem to have balance in their life. I love this analogy, because it mirrors the real estate business.

I know a lot of people may be struggling, and you may be one of them. There is no shortcut in this business to the amount of work that is involved to get it off the ground — it must be intentional and focused. You have to employ specific strategies at specific times. *Every* effort, *every* activity, *every* connection, *every* bit of marketing, *every* contact, *every* sale, *every* listing, *everything* has to build on itself to ensure lift off. Efficiency, traction and momentum — all have to be employed at the same time. If you don't, you won't get your business to lift off. You will run out of runway. This is where people quit. They run out of resources. They run of energy. They run out of money. They run out of time. They run out of patience. They run out. But the interesting thing is: this failure to lift off is usually because the real estate agent wasn't running at all—at least, not at full speed. So, you need to be going full blast but with concentrated effort and all wheels turning in the right direction and all engines going.

Keep the Tank Full.

I am talking about your brain. This is where you need to keep the mind sharp and focussed on your business. Fill your mind with information that will serve you and serve your clients. Don't get bogged down with media information, negativity and "fail videos," or cute cat videos. War stories from other agents in your office will not serve you well. Don't get caught up in rants or complaints from some political figure or some person in your community. Just focus on what you need to know that helps you to serve others. Keep it simple.

Fill your brain with market knowledge. View a lot of homes. Get a clear understanding of pricing. Multiple times per day, you should be checking new listings and sales and keeping yourself abreast of market conditions. Become a specialist in your area. In addition, create a routine of "feeding the brain" with lots of nourishing information that serves you and puts you in the right mindset to prepare you for success. Do this first thing in the morning and again before you go to sleep, so your mind percolates on that information all night long. You will notice a difference in the first week. Keep the tank full.

Also, you should invest in good information that will help you understand what to do, in order to keep the throttle down. But make sure it is good information that gives you clarity. Don't get fooled by the new "easy thing" — the "one thing" that people tell you will make you successful. The truth is, there is never "one thing." Who you are today and how your brain works today, the habits that dominate your life and your mind, all came from years of input. Many things.

Success in this business comes from a combination of many skills, habits and conditions: your mental capacity, your beliefs (that are either serving you or holding you back), your insecurities and quirks. There is no one thing that has made you into who you are today, you are made up of many things. Our habits and thought patterns, make us who we are and that state was not developed overnight. So, we have to intentionally interrupt the status quo and work on ourselves, so that we constantly move towards becoming the best version of ourselves. Keeping yourself educated and informed is what professionals do. Learn and improve constantly, so that you get to the point of knowing with absolute certainty that when you get that chance to meet someone, you will win the business.

Professionals know the value of their mind. You have to protect your mind as if your life depends on it, because it does. The other benefit of this is that you begin to create a concrete belief. Belief is what will define your success. Your level of success is in direct correlation to your level of belief. Keep the tank full.

Don't Rely on Your Dot

What is your dot? Your dot is your Sphere of Influence. People think that their sphere of influence is bigger than it really is. It's funny. I hear it all the time. "I just know so many people that I thought that real estate would be good for me." If they know you too well, how do you think that will work out for you? Think back to grade seven, when you made fun of Susie and her braided hair. What about just out of high school when you were a little intoxicated and did something stupid? What about at your last job when you were gossiping with your buddy about another person?

Everybody has a past. Most of us have done things that we are not proud of. All of your past stuff will kick you in the butt. If you were totally perfect in your past (which is not the case for most people), then maybe your sphere of influencer will work out very well for you. But it's still a dot.

Got a big family? Sure, family members can be good for business. But, normally, they expect a discount, right? And, in truth, they only germinate deals once in a while. Your sphere of influence, your "dot," can help for a little while and possibly be responsible for a few deals a year, but it won't be able to support your business. You need to create a pipeline of leads that are constantly entering your atmosphere.

Your little dot needs to expand its influence and affect other dots. These other dots are very, very, very, important to your success. They each have their own gravitational pull by attracting other people they know and directing them to you. This is where business gets fun.

One of the first things that new agents are taught by mentors, trainers, and coaches, is to expand their Sphere of Influence. This is partly correct, in my opinion. You definitely want to tap into that right away. If you allow me, I just want to alter the mindset slightly. The challenge with that is they visualize expanding one finite circle. Instead of connecting infinite dots. That's the difference. Your world of influence, or "sphere of influence" is nothing more than a dot. Accept that. The sooner you realize that, the better. Picture a circle. Now picture many dots. They spend a bunch of money attempting to expand their own circle or sphere, by throwing marketing dollars at increasing their presence. In the end, they end of up sacrificing all of the other dots around them that could have done a much better job of marketing for them. Focus on the dots, man. Focus on the dots. You have to get outside of your own sense of importance and serve others well, and then they will help you build your business. Picture this: On a clear night, you can look up in the sky and see the moon. Imagine it is a full moon. It is bright and much more noticeable than the millions of stars in the sky. You see, this is the first instinct that Real Estate professionals act upon. To make themselves look bigger and brighter. They want to be like the moon. Some people are very good at this and it works for them. My theory is that, it takes a lot of money to keep your Moon looking brighter than all of the other competition. Focus on the stars. There are many more stars in the sky. Each one has its own gravitational pull. You will notice that stars sometimes cluster together. The stars represent other people. Many people who will introduce you to other stars. People will refer people to other people who they relate to. People that they trust. People that aren't trying to be more important than them. That is the best analogy that I can think of. Instead of focusing on your own "brightness" or "importance", focus on making those stars important and they will in turn, bring people into your world, for you on your behalf.

Obey the Two Laws

The Law of Sowing and Reaping. The Law of Reciprocity. These are laws. They are not theories or neat little ideas. They are not just good Pinterest quotes, or a business philosophy wall hanging. They are laws. The law of gravity is an example of a similar law. If you jump off the roof of your house, you will fall downwards, and it will most likely hurt. It is non-negotiable, just like The Law of Sowing and Reaping and The Law of Reciprocity. People who understand the power of these laws are successful. Full stop.

Both of these laws boil down to one concept — you've got to give, before you get. Simple as that. Most people have a 'what's in it for me,' kind of attitude. *They* want to see what they can get away with. I have personally witnessed, many agents, trying to figure out the minimum amount of effort to get the maximum benefit for themselves. Not you. Let *everyone* else operate that way. It creates more opportunities for you! People notice the difference. You want more and more dots, right? Create raving fans. Let those raving fans, do the marketing for you. They will. This is the secret to building a great business.

The Law of Sowing and Reaping gives me a sense of calm. You know why? Because it is something that I can control. I can plant seeds, ideas, and goodwill with people. I can create opportunities. I can find ways to help people. I can give good advice. I can be an advocate for them. I can give them market knowledge. I can be a positive force in their lives. I can protect them contractually. I can help them make a great decision. Those things are in my control.

What is out of my control? Who gets elected president, the weather, natural disasters that happen, or virus, that we can't even see with our naked eyes, sweeping the world and putting everything on pause for a while. I can't control bank interest rates or government policy. I can't control when someone wants to retire and buy into another area, or when a first-time buyer has saved enough money to buy a home, or when that person will get married or have children. I can't control any of those things, but all of those things influence our industry and our businesses.

What I *can* do, is plant seeds of positivity and give people information. I can help them prepare for when the time is

right and give them good information to rely upon, in o
to make a great plan for their lives and their family. I ca
a trusted resource for them, and I can inspire them, so t
will want to send business my way. These actions are all under my control.

The Law of Reciprocity is another one. I can direct people to others' businesses or help others by referring people to them. My actions help them out and then suddenly, one day, that person may refer someone to me. I make sure that I do a good job and then I have inadvertently inspired them to send business my way again. I can control that. When I think outside of myself and find a way to be of benefit to others, with no conditions or expectations , business suddenly comes to me--from the strangest places and at the most unexpected times.

Recap on the Four Mindsets

Full Throttle: Keep the pedal to the metal and get your business to lift off.

Keep the Tank Full: Be a student of the business and the industry and in a constant mode of self-improvement.

Don't Rely on Your Dot: It's a hard truth. But you are going to leave your zone of comfort. The good news is, you will enrich your life with new friends who you would never have met had you not left that zone. It's awesome.

Obey and Integrate These Two Laws into your daily lives: The Law of Sowing and Reaping and the Law of Reciprocity.

MINDSET MASTERY, PART ONE

The following section is foundational to Attracting, Attaining, Serving and Retaining Business. Yes...all four parts of the 4X Agent is affected by Mindset Mastery. Approaching each area with these mindsets will set you leap years ahead of your competition.

"Successful people are always looking for opportunities to help others. Unsuccessful people are always asking 'what's in it for me?'"
—Brian Tracy

I believe that this quote from Brian Tracy, a well-known sales trainer, tackles both the external and the internal mindsets.

Successful people focus on helping people get what they want, by filling a need, solving a problem or meeting a challenge. The number of people you help is in direct proportion to the amount of money that you will earn in your life.

Mindsets for Dealing with People

Part 1 – External – What are the external mindsets that we need to understand with absolute clarity in order to enjoy the Dream Real Estate Business?

We are going to cover the Six Critical Mindset Principles:

1. We are Dealing with People
2. The Trust Account
3. Help People Get What They Want
4. Gain the Advantage by Understanding Personality Types
5. Relational Versus Transactional Thinking
6. Every Person is an Opportunity

Principle #1: Dealing with People

We are dealing with people. People. I know this sounds so obvious; it's not really earth-shattering news. But I think many people who get into real estate are afraid of people. Our world is changing. Neighbourhoods are changing. The fact that, in most cases, both the husband and the wife have to work now, is changing the household dynamic. Buying habits are evolving. People are getting very comfortable online. The various ways we can communicate with people are changing. Personal contact is diminishing. The fact that we can market to people in so many different types of mediums is changing how we communicate value.

This is creating a lot of noise. A lot of distractions. We are bombarded with so many different types of messages now.

But, deep down, there is this unchanging need. We prefer to deal with people. That's it.

How many times have you called a 1-800 number and went through all of the prompts to get a certain result and become increasingly frustrated because you simply wanted to talk to a real live person?

How many times have you had a need that didn't fit with the computer-generated prompts and were left frustrated. It's infuriating, right?

But we also have a fear of being judged by people. We have fears about rejection. We worry about "being sold" or "being taken advantage of." Do you relate to that? That's because we are all people, dealing with people. We all have the same concerns. What do people dislike?

Well, if *you* dislike certain tactics, there is a good chance that your "prospects" feel the same. Do *you* like being "baited" into doing things? Do *you* like being taken advantage of? Does anybody enjoy that? Do *you* enjoy doing business with someone because they guilted you into it? Do you sometimes have reservations and trust issues with other people, that is, until they prove their trustworthiness? Do we enjoy being treated like a number? Do we like getting a phone call from a "Lead Source" company? Do we like getting calls from companies like "Vegas Vacations" offering us a crazy deal that we have to pay for today without having a chance to check things out? I call these strategies "using the MATRIX approach" to get leads. It's like casting a net in the water to catch fish without using the proper bait. It's just catching a bunch of fish that haphazardly swim into the net area.

Does anybody enjoy being one of those "caught in the net"? **Fundamentally,** everyone has a back story. It's undeniable that every single person you come into contact with has a different frame of reference than you. Their FEARS are real. So, when you first come into contact with people, think about who you are to them**.** Consider their perspective. We are in an age now where people want to choose carefully who they let into their inner circle.

Think about your **Negative** past experiences with others throughout your life:

- Have you ever experienced a service providers or salesperson you disliked?
- Has someone ever let you down?
- Have people ever lied to you?
- Have you ever dealt with a sales rep who was less than impressive or didn't live up to what they claimed to be?

Now think about your **Positive** past experiences with others:

- Have you ever felt that you truly needed another person or professional as a trustworthy confidant?
- Have you ever dealt with someone who "wowed" you? They just blew your mind.
- Have you ever dealt with someone who went above and beyond the call of duty?
- Have you ever dealt with a professional who was totally in your corner?
- Have you ever had a professional in your life you could totally trust?

Don't you agree we should all strive to be the kind of person that we would most likely like to deal with? So then, become that. Become that person. Ultimately, this is what I believe a 4X Agent is. And you are on your way to being that.

First Step: Once you understand the frame of reference a person is coming from, you become un-offendable. We are such sensitive souls, aren't we?

The world is all about not offending anyone. It's about being careful to use the right words to describe people. We wear certain coloured shirts on certain days of the year, and we wrap ribbons, and we paint sidewalks to create "acceptance for all!" What if we were not offendable? What if we were not offendable because we accepted everyone? Their back stories. Their differences. Their personal challenges, fears and struggles, Their economic status, Their lifestyle choices, Their skin color, Their choice of Religion or Their political beliefs. If everyone did that then we would all be okay. We wouldn't have to create all of these "movements" and "demonstrations." I won't go too deep on this, because I know there are challenges out there that are much bigger and the solutions are more complicated, but my overarching point on this subject boils down to this: ...Be un-offendable.

What we're discussing right now is frame of reference. I am not sure how many people are reading this book at this moment, but I know this. Each one of you internalized the positive and negative questions that I just posed...differently. Each one of you responded to those statements, in your own unique way. So simply understand that. Every one of those issues affect you in some way. You have your own frame of reference on those issues and so does someone else. Choose grace, understanding and empathy in all areas of your life. Try not to offend someone else, and try to be unoffendable.

There is no *one size fits all* type of marketing. No action, or script, or slick website will satisfy all people in the same way. All we can do is simply embrace the fact that we are all different and we all have past experiences that have got us here today. And that fact is absolutely true for the people that you come into contact with in your business every day, every time, in every circumstance.

Before habitually being offended (which is the truth, by the way; being offended is a habit), I encourage you to consider the frame of reference and figure out how you can **be what that person needs**, by asking the right questions and earning their trust.

That brings us to principle #2:

Principle #2: The Trust Account

I can sum up his one pretty simply: ***"Earn their trust as quickly as you can, and then, NEVER betray it"*** Okay...do you get it? Should we move on to Principle #3...? No, this one is worth talking about for a bit.

Years ago, I had a chat with my kids about bank accounts. We were talking about being responsible with money. My daughter had started to do a lot of babysitting around our neighbourhood and was beginning to make a pretty good income for a 13-year-old girl. I thought it was a good time to chat about managing finances, saving money, and how bank accounts work.

Then this little light bulb came on while we were talking about how bank accounts work, and I segued into a discussion about what I referred to as "The Trust Account."

The idea of deposits and withdrawals is what triggered this little light bulb. The discussion went like this:

"When we ask you a question and you tell us the truth, you are effectively making deposits into our TRUST account. If we trust you to get something done for us to help out around the house, and you complete that task, you are effectively making deposits into our TRUST account. We start to trust you more and more. We, as your parents, don't want to have to micromanage everything. We want to be able to ask you to do something or not do something and then we don't want to have to worry about whether we can trust you to abide by that agreement. So, as we go through life together these things will happen and as you continue to do what you say...the Trust Account Builds up because an increasing number of deposits have been made.

"But there is a flip-side. If you *don't* do what was agreed or don't do it well, to the best of your ability, then no deposits are being made. If we catch you in a lie, a withdrawal is made by default. If there are continuous withdrawals happening with no deposits, then we can never trust you. Nobody wants that. We want to be able to trust you.

"Sometimes you will mess up," I told my kids. "You will make a mistake or there will be a misunderstanding on what was agreed. That will happen. But if no deposits are made, it is hard to trust. Even if it is an honest mistake that particular time. But if the Trust Account has a good balance in there from past deposits then there is something to withdraw. Our trust with each other remains intact.

"As your parents, we will do the same thing," I continued. "When I say I am going to do something for you, do you have any doubt in your minds? Do you wonder if Daddy will do what he says this time?"

The children all agreed that their answer was no, and I went on.

"So, I have effectively made some deposits in your Trust account already right? So, if one day I get mixed up and get the time wrong or forget something because I'm human and I mess up sometimes, then you will trust that it was an honest mistake and not a case where I neglected to be true to my word. Right?"

That whole conversation happened off the cuff at the time, but I love that analogy. But does it make sense to you?

What if we apply that principal into our businesses? What if that is our first goal when we meet someone? What if this was the first question that entered our minds: "How do I earn their trust quickly?" How can I begin making deposits into this person's TRUST ACCOUNT as quickly as possible?

The wonderful thing about questions, is that our minds naturally begin to search for answers to them. That is one of the things that separates us from animals and makes us a superior species. We instinctively ask questions and then search for answers...

We just have to be very intentional about the questions that we ask, to ourselves and to others.

"How do I earn someone's trust quickly?" Is a very powerful question. If you ask that question, you will never need to manipulate, fool or trick people into doing business with you.

Here is the other reason the trust account is so important. Real estate professionals are still in the top five for Least Trusted Professionals in the United States It is truly a SAD Fact. I do believe that we are gaining ground and people are beginning to associate the word "REALTOR®" with the idea of a valuable and trusted resource. But there are other business models fighting against us. There are even different business models out there now that are attempting to eliminate the REALTOR® altogether. Some real estate critics are trying to make a case for the fact that we are not relevant to the process. This is a fight that we need to take on. More than ever, we have to get really good at communicating and proving our value and building a foundation of trust with the general public.

I think that we have a lot of work to do as an Industry. This is your first goal from your very first interaction with another person, in all areas of your life. Seek to build trust and then never betray that trust. Build trust. But how do we do that?

Here are 7 steps you can take immediately to start making deposits in your clients' trust accounts:

1. Listen intently and learn what is important to them.
2. Feed the information back to them to summarize.
3. Give suggestions on how you can help them focus on their dream.
4. Commit to doing something for them that will be helpful.
5. Do it. Do it well. Do it when you said you were going to do it.
6. Follow up to ensure that you are the right track.
7. Ask how to help again...give suggestions...thank them.

Principle #3: Help People Get What They Want

What do your clients want? Determine what that is, then help them get it. Simple, Right...?

Funny, but here is what complicates things: US, the real estate agents. We get in the way sometimes.

I know you may need this sale. Now. I get it. You may be in emergency mode right now, maybe even behind on your mortgage payment right now. You may be in dire financial circumstances, and the stress is mounting. You may be desperate to close a transaction and you need this person to make a decision and close as quickly as possible.

I understand, but I am sorry to say...IT IS NOT ABOUT YOU...IT WILL NEVER BE ABOUT YOU. Stage One of the relationship has to be totally focused on the client:

100% focus on their needs, wants and desires

100% focus on their challenges and how to overcome them

100% focus on finding ways to be of value to them

100% focus on earning their trust

This is not the time to tell people how great you are. In many ways, you have no right to even ask for their phone number or email until they know that you have their best interests in mind. That's the truth of the matter. I am not suggesting that you should not attempt to get this information if you can. But I maintain that you actually don't really have a *right* to that information until you have fulfilled the first stage of the relationship. You must earn that right. First, focus outwardly instead of inwardly. Sometimes we can be overly concerned with our own insecurities. We forget to simply be human beings seeking to understand another human being. The instinct is to "present" a specific type of persona to people and "sell" them on our worth. But we don't have to do this at all. If we simply follow Step One and *help people get what they want*, they will be happy and excited to give us their contact information because they receive some sort of value for doing so. They will be convinced that you are the best person to help them. It is easier than you think but for some people, this is a major mindset shift.

"People don't care how much you know until they know how much you care"
-Theodore Roosevelt

Here is another quotation that says the same thing in a different but more practical way from Trish Bertuzzi, founder and CEO of The Bridge Group, Sales Consultants

"Prospects are making their purchase decision based on whether they think you understand their problems and you have the knowledge, resources, and commitment to solving them."
-Trish Bertuzzi

So, how do you accomplish that? By being interested in them. By focusing on discovering, and uncovering information that will give you clues, on their needs, wants and desires. We are so wrapped up in our own insecurities. Some of us have imposter syndrome. We see how successful agents act and begin to mimic them. We convince ourselves, that we need to create some sort of character or persona to people to "sell" them on the fact that we are the best choice for them. But the truth is, we don't have to convince them we are worthy. All we have to do is to listen to them. If we're talking the whole time, at them, instead of asking them intelligent questions *about* them, how are we going to figure out how to help them?

So, essentially:

You don't have to convince them that you are worthy, they will convince themselves of that fact if you put their needs first.

Get them talking about themselves: IT'S THE SUBJECT THEY KNOW BEST. For example, here are 10 questions for a typical family that you would meet in an open house:

1. What are your needs in a home?
2. Are you upsizing? Or relocating?
3. Where do you work? In town? Out of town?
4. Do you have children?
5. What are the kids' age ranges?
6. Do you want to be close to schools?
7. Do you commute to work?
8. Do both spouses work?
9. Where are you living presently? What's the scenario? Renting? Owners?
10. How long have you been there?

If you were able to garner answers from these 10 questions, would you be able to provide some solutions for this particular target market? Seek to understand.

Watch the Transformation

From strangers to unmet friends to clients to friends to referral sources; That's the ultimate transformation that you are hoping for in your relationship with people you have just met.

But how about the transformation that occurs in the 10 to 15 minutes that you are with them?

It's amazing how intelligent you sound to people when you are talking to them and offering solutions that are custom fit to them. You transform in their eyes from a "salesy salesperson" to simply a "nice person." Okay...first goal achieved. Now you have graduated to a longer conversation with them. You learn more about them, you offer a solution for them, you go from Salesy Salesperson to Nice Person to *someone who knows what they're talking about. Then* you ask more questions, learn more about them, then you communicate to them how you can help them if they like. You ask permission. Now, they want to know more about how you can help them, you have become a "solutions provider" for them, someone who is in their corner, their advocate...

WATCH THEIR BODY LANGUAGE. The clues are obvious, once you become conscious of them.

This is a skill that needs to be developed. Remember, we are dealing with *people*. Being able to "read" people is so important. A computer program cannot do it. An Internet LEAD CATCHER cannot do it. This is part of the process that is unique to human beings.

You can literally watch people's body language and begin to understand if you have achieved some form of trust in the exchange. People will be guarded and curt and trying not to look you in the eyes but then, suddenly, they are leaning in, looking you in the eyes, nodding their head in agreement and understanding. When that happens, you know you have made a connection...a human connection. Even on the telephone in a conversation you can hear the difference in the voice. Once they feel relaxed, they will begin to tell you much more about themselves and--when you offer solutions, or ideas, or offer to do something for them--you will hear excitement, and sometimes surprise in their voice. This is when you know you have made a human connection. Trust is starting to be built.

Achievement Unlocked! This is the first step. This is the beginning of it all.

Principle #4 – People are Different

It's essential to figure out how to relate to people. One way to gain advantage is by understanding personality types.

Although there are many different variations of personality types out there, I believe that there are four basic qualities that our clients expect of us. I call these the Four Basic Requirements. Believe it or not...some real estate agents don't even meet these four basic requirements. So, as a minimum standard, here are the four areas where you need to be consistent to satisfy the public's basic standards:

1. We need to be trustworthy, to earn someone's trust and then never betray it.
2. We need to communicate well. This is a common issue with most professionals. People want you to return their phone calls, emails and texts in a timely manner, providing a weekly report on the listing.
3. We need to be results driven. The client wants to know that you are doing everything possible to get their desired result.
4. We need to be capable and professional. They want to know that you are a student of the business. That you are committed. They want to feel like they are in good hands, and that you take this assignment seriously.

The primacy of these four qualities holds true, in some degree, to people in all walks of life. In a nutshell, this is what most people want from us. Understanding how to be professional and meeting the expectations of most people is crucial, for sure. Later on in this book, we'll discuss systems and give you some tools to excel at this skill.

But what about the understanding the nuances of personality types? This is the competitive edge that makes the greatest difference in the success of your business. This is where your business will soar to new heights. Most highly successful agents aren't even aware that they are skilled in these nuances, believe it or not.

We real estate professionals aren't screened out by personality type, so there are over two million of us running around out there. If you put us all into one city, the varying degrees of personality types would become abundantly clear. Imagine that? A bunch of real estate agents all in one place, having to co-habit together? What a social experiment that would be...

So, is it possible that we are going to "rub people the wrong way" sometimes? Will some people grind on us or aggravate us a bit? Is it possible? Yes. Is it possible that there will be certain people who we really seem to connect with, and enjoy working with? Sure. But that will be a small few because we all think so differently.

That is why it is so important to cover the next topic: Increasing our level of tolerance and understanding, so that we serve people where their needs are. Remember...it's not about us. It's about them.

There are quite a few studies out there that tackle personality types. Some are: the *DISC Method*, the *Meyers-Briggs Method,* the *Jungian Method.* One method is simply called, the Four Personality Types. There is even one method that involves colours.

So, with all of these options, how do we solve the personality type puzzle?

One way is to create a tolerance and an understanding of an unfamiliar personality type. Give yourself a new habit that involves going into that mindset. Just doing that will allow you to increase your ability to empathize with people in a more nuanced way.

I would suggest that you pick one of these profiling systems and do it for yourself. Learn about yourself. Don't pigeon-hole yourself. Just forming a better understanding of your own tendencies will help you to be better equipped to serve others at the level they need to be served. The goal is not to become a personality profile specialist, but investing some time on this will help you better attract more people into your world of dots. It will go a long way to building trust. It will give you a better chance of creating successful outcomes for your business. Every interaction is a chance for business.

Now discuss the next challenge.

People are different. But then you have to add some other ingredients that *really* mess things up:

- ☐ What about their past experiences?
- ☐ How does that form their frame of reference?
- ☐ What is the desired outcome that they are trying to achieve? Is it realistic? Is it based on outer influences that you still need to discover?

Here are a few examples of personality types you are likely to run into:

There is the **"*Where-Do-I-Sign*?-Guy." T**his is a person who is not really listening to you as you talk about all the details and nuances of the contract. "Yeah, yeah," he'll say. "Stop talking. Where do I sign? I'm busy and I have things to do." For people like this, get to the point quicker and move on to the next step. If you are a detailed-oriented personality type, this will be hard for you, but you need to recognize this person for who they are and operate at a level that is important to them.

There is the **Detail-Oriented Person**. These people want lots of data. They want to be armed with information. Their comfort zone is knowing all of the details. This will aggravate you if you are not like this person, if you are more of a blue-sky kind of "big picture" kind of thinker. To you, that minor minutia is not really that important in the scheme of things. But again, it is not about you. This person's WOW is how amazing you are at getting information to them in a timely manner. Yes, it is more work but that is the WOW to them. Dropping off a gift knife set to them after the sale won't impress them as much as you'd think it should. However, diligently providing them with complete and organized details and data will impress them.

Then there is the **"EMOTIONAL Touch-Feely" Person**. This person uses language that is all about how things feel. They are always telling you how they feel about things. Listen for those word cues in their language: "I feel like we have seen this one before..." "This home just doesn't feel right to me..." ... "I really felt like that person wasn't listening to me..."

These people will remember an experience by how they felt during it. They buy mostly on emotion. They might get disappointed easily, so it is important to empathize with their feelings. Spend extra energy with these people, placating their feelings. Another thing I have noticed about this personality type is that they miss the details of your message when you are speaking to them because they are so focused on how they are feeling at the time. Sometimes *one word* will cause them to mentally go on a little trip and they will not hear the rest of the sentence. You have to be very diligent in reinforcing what you have told them in other ways. Send an email summarizing what you spoke about and use a lot of language that involves emotion, telling them how excited you are to help them.

There are some clients who don't hear your words and internalize understanding as fast as you are talking. Sometimes you have to adjust your tone. Sometimes you have to adjust your speed. Slow down for them. If they are looking at you with glossed-over eyes and you notice some tension on their face, they might need time to process. Give them time. Talk softer and slower. Don't get into too many onerous details. Keep the message simple. Re-phrase something you just said in straightforward terms until you see them relax their face and nod in understanding.

The biggest message I have here is to simply be aware. Be aware. Be present in the moment. Forget about your own stuff, it is not about you. It is about that person. *You need to be who they need you to be, for those moments.*

All of these efforts have an enormous influence in the real estate business. This is stuff that is not taught in the office. This is something that all successful agents practice at some level and they wouldn't even know that they are doing it.

They are doing it instinctively, but you can learn to hone these skills and take your business to the next level.

Mindset Principle #5: Relational Versus Transactional

Let's break down these terms. What's the difference?

We are dealing with people, not robots. I think I have made a pretty strong case for this up to this point. I hope I have convinced you of it. And if you have any real estate experience by now, you haven't had to help a robot buy a home. "So, Captain Obvious," you're probably thinking. " What are you talking about then?"

Here's my beef. When I Google "Lead Generation for REALTORS®" I get pages and pages of companies that do this service. After the eleventh page there are still PAID ads on Google. After the *eleventh page!* People are paying to show up on the page that never gets looked at—page 11!! Are you kidding me?

This tells me that a lot of real estate agents are buying leads from companies advertising on Google to make a living in real estate. In my opinion, they are vultures, preying on the weak. Now, I am not totally against utilizing every advantage possible in order to create a great business but here's my point.

Let's assume that when you receive a lead, and then contact that lead, the person you call is going to be happy to hear from you. But they are never "pre-qualified" and sorted and ready for your call. Never. If the lead supplier has promised you otherwise, it is a lie. Or it will be much more expensive.

A warm lead comes from a real estate pro who 1) is very good on the phone, 2) understands the mindsets of personality types, 3) knows the neighborhood in question, 4) has had a high quality conversation with that "lead", or person, determining their needs, wants, desires and plan and 5) is hot and ready to do something within the next 30 to 90 days. That is a warm lead. If it isn't a warm lead, you have to ask the question: Is this worth paying for?

Maybe, it's worth something If you have a system and are armed with knowledge and can find a way to get through that "sales barrier" on the phone. But I will tell you from personal experience and testing with agents that the conversion rate is very low. The reason? People are not robots.

Just because someone was curious about a listing, clicked on it and was forced to fill out a form in order to get more info, does not make them a pre-qualified lead. Sure...one 1 in 20 may be a hot buyer, but then divide that by the number of those people who were actually already working with agents but were searching in their free time on a Saturday evening. The lead impact diminishes greatly...

Until they receive a phone call from you, there is no human interaction for this potential client. They are a robot, which has been pushed through an algorithm and ended up in your inbox because you paid to be the one agent in the area to receive those leads. [I do a whole episode on this subject, called "Do You Want 100 Leads Per Month?," in Season 2, Episode 27 of my podcast *4X Formula Real Estate Training]*.

A 4X Agent Builds Relationships

That is a mindset. It's what you are, or what you are to become. You just simply ARE a person who builds relationships. Remember this? We need to get out of the top five LEAST TRUSTED and move up into the MOST TRUSTED category...that is our mission.

For me, internet lead generation can be summed up in this image: You just cast a net and pull in what gets caught in the net.

There are a couple of challenges here: 1) They are all casting their nets in the same body of water. 2) They catch a lot of things in that net. A lot of fish in the net are the ones that ou don't want. You can spend a lot of time on the sorting. And you are paying for this?

You cannot automate human beings. That is what gives us our relevance as real estate professionals: We are humans dealing with humans and that is the essence.

But what if we created an team of people out there fishing for us? For free! They would be fishing in pools of water all over the place, using the correct bait. Remember the dots? Imagine that those dots are people, and that they're everywhere, and they're working for you.

I'm talking about relationships. Once you have a relationship, there is no more sorting through a bunch of unwanted stuff. That is a powerful business. This is a business that will withstand all market conditions, one that runs more efficiently and is highly profitable.

So, with all of that in mind...how should we refer to the people that we serve?

A customer is **Transactional.** Customers buy cars, furniture and groceries. But that's it. On the other hand, a *client* utilizes the services of a professional who values them. This is a **Relational** connection. It grinds on me like a scratchy record player or fingernails on a chalkboard when I hear people talk about their sellers or buyers as "customers."

We have a database of **clients** that we serve, not a list of customers that we sell houses to. Do you agree with me on that? I hope so. That one mindset alone can change your business.

Have you heard the saying, **"The customer is always right?"**

Well, I am here to tell you: "My clients are not always right." They aren't. Because I am the professional. I do this for a living. This is all I think about every day. I know my marketplace. I know the dynamics of how buyers think. I would not be doing my clients a favor if I held them up as "always right." It is my job to help guide and, actually, help protect them from themselves sometimes. I have to look out for their best interests at all times, and sometimes that means I have to tell them —in a sensitive and professional way —when they are not correct. Sometimes, my clients require a tactful adjustment to their thinking. But I can only do that when I have earned their trust.

How would you like to be referred to? Here are some choices:

"**MY** REALTOR®", "**MY** REAL ESTATE PROFESSIONAL," or "**MY** REAL ESTATE AGENT." All three phrases invoke a relationship.

Or...

"THE REALTOR®", "**THE** REAL ESTATE AGENT" or, even worse: "**THAT** REALTOR® OR **THAT** LISTING AGENT." What does this title suggest? A service provider? A necessary evil? Somebody no one really knows or cares to know?

Which brings us to:

Mindset Principle #6 – Every Single Person You Come into Contact With is an Opportunity for Business.

Think about all of the people who you come into contact with on a daily, weekly, monthly and yearly basis. In every circumstance that you are out and about, there are other people you have the opportunity to interact with.

Let's form a list: the Starbucks drive-through, buying a car, buying a suit, bringing your kids to their soccer practice, a school concert, talking with a neighbour, at the gas station, in a restaurant, picking up your dry-cleaning, at church, at the job site checking out new construction, talking to the secretary at your accounting office, talking to the people who work in the office next to your office,

at the city or county office, getting a permit.

Think about every one of those interactions. Are you proud of how you conduct yourself? Do you think that when you leave, anyone who you come into contact with feels any more self-worth than the last person that they interacted with? Do you think they will remember you the next time you see them? Do you give them a good reason to remember you?

Focus on this. They are not just handing you your coffee. They are people, with real jobs and unspoken dreams. They may not be buying a home today, but they know somebody who is. Let me rephrase that...do you know if they are looking to buy or sell a home today? How do you know? Engage everyone. Be memorable. Leave a positive impression. Plant a positive seed and see if one day it germinates. Nothing bad can come of this.

Your waitress, who maybe looks like she can't afford to buy a home, could meet a guy tomorrow and six months from today be looking for a home. The drywaller on the job site could be close to saving enough money to buy his first home. Or maybe his wife has parents with money who want to help them get into a home. You never know. Make friends. Make contacts. Make people feel worthy of your conversation and time. It doesn't take much. How many potential opportunities are missed every single day? We will never know.

How do you like to be treated?

Consider this scenario: You have a listing. Someone calls you up. They want to view your listing. They are just curious, doing research. You are the listing agent, so you are the one they call to view the home. You get in your car, drive over to the listing and show them the home. They don't want to give you any information and everyone leaves and goes their separate ways after the showing. You never speak to them again.

Has this ever happened to you? Well, we will deal with this situation later on in the course. But it does happen.

So...who were you to those people, in that situation? were a "door opener." That was your role. To open the for this other person to look at the home. That's it. That is what you were to them: a means to an end.

How does that make you feel?

Well, that is kind of how we are making other people feel. They are just fulfilling a certain role for us; we don't deem them important enough to engage in a deeper human interaction.

Make human connections throughout your days at every point of contact. This is a new habit that you will pack into your daily life now. Eventually, it will be the key to your success. Making human connections is another one of those successful traits and activities that successful people practice. Normally, they practice this habit instinctively. They just do it.

Okay, so we have covered the Six Critical Mindset Principles on how to approach the people we serve. This is the outward focus. Putting into practice these mindsets will ensure that you will succeed in real estate. The very fact that we are *people dealing with people* is the reason that we will always be relevant. We cannot be replaced. There is an opposing force out there that is saying that we can be replaced. But remember this: An algorithm will not replace you as long as you create more relevance by making this your core belief: We are PEOPLE who HELP people.

In order to do that, we have to create some sort of relationship. Relationships have levels of intensity. We don't always kiss on the first date. We have to earn the trust, help them get what they want..., that each person has different needs and different ways of interpreting what is important to them. Treat every single person as an opportunity in some small way. We need to understand that our clients are impressed by very different WOW factors; our job is to figure out which

WOW FACTOR is important to them, not what we THINK should be important to them.

Focus on these elements and implement them into your daily practice and watch what happens. Create new habits and thought patterns to implement these elements and you will not be able to stop it once it gets going!!

Congratulations! This concludes Part One of Mindset Mastery. Part Two deals with the internal mindsets we all need to master in order to create massive and sustainable success in our real estate businesses.

MINDSET MASTERY, PART TWO

Internal Mindsets for Success

First things first: you need to ditch the "employee mentality." You do not work FOR anyone. You don't work FOR a brokerage; you work WITH them. Instead, you work for the client. That mindset alone will steer your mentality to the right place.

You are a "REALTOR®-PRENEUR," a licensed real estate professional who is an entrepreneur. You are building and running a business. You are the CEO, the CFO, the COO, the Marketing Department, the Service Department, Head of Communications, Branding, and don't forget – the secretary and the janitor.

At first, you will have to be all of these roles. Later, you master them. Still later on your journey, as you enjoy more cash flow, you can plug other people into these roles as you progress.

YOU, INC.

So, what does that mean? You. Nobody else is to blame for your success or failure. Nobody. Only you. You, Incorporated.

You can't blame your brokerage, your upbringing, your family life, your competition, your current mayor, the conflict in Iran or Iraq...or the latest tweet from ex-President Donald Trump. None of that matters.

Once that is established then you move forward from that platform.

So, even if you have left a J-O-B to become a real estate agent and have joined a reputable brokerage you have chosen based on a) what they are going to do for you, b) the number of mentors in the office, or c) any other criteria that allows you to off-load the responsibility of your success to a 3rd party, you can't forget this mindset: *You, Inc* will succeed or fail on <u>your</u> watch.

This is really important. This is the foundation to your thinking and everything else we talk about will springboard off of this.

This responsibility may actually freak some of you out. It may fire some of you up. All of that is okay. My goal by the end of Part Two is that you will be excited and empowered by the thought that you are in control.

I need to clarify something: Picking a real estate firm based on various criteria that are important to you is perfectly acceptable. If your office provides a lot of support, that is good. But these are bonuses. I want you to be thinking in terms of the REALTOR®-PRENEUR ideal, that's all.

The buck stops here, at you. Once you begin to have confidence in your own abilities, you begin to set different criteria when making a decision for the type of office that you need. If your mindset is already in a place where your self-talk sounds like, "I know what I can do," and "I know that I have a plan," or "I know my work habits and I have systems in place to do the amount of business that I want to do," and "I need to find an office that will leverage and multiply my business." See how empowering that is?

You are a business within a business. Believe it or not, you can be way more profitable than the business that you are operating in. For certain. Your *Expense to Profit* ratio has far more potential for increasing the spread as you increase your business over time, utilizing the 4XFormula Quick Commission Accelerator Course.

Here is a quote from one of the best success trainers who ever lived:

"Let others lead small lives, but not you...Let others argue over small things, but not you...Let others cry over small hurts, but not you...Let others leave their future in someone else's hands, but not you."
— Jim Rohn

Embrace this mindset and begin to own everything.

So, now that you fully understand that you are a business within a business, do you believe that you are in the BEST business, a GREAT business, a business that maximizes your potential?

If there is any doubt in your mind right now, then we need to take care of that next.

WHAT is so great about the REAL ESTATE BUSINESS?

I am going to talk about Five Reasons why helping people buy and sell homes is a great business

1. **Creativity Expands**

A lot of businesses are reliant on traffic coming through the door. They rely on old-school ways of attracting business. In some cases, their business is focused on a very specific need, so they have limited ability to be creative. Or maybe you have noticed that, in a J-O-B, you are there to fulfill what you are being told to do, trading your time for money. That is a situation where our Creativity Muscles get flabby. In real estate we get to flex those muscles and exercise creativity on a daily basis.

Where do we exercise Creativity?

- ☐ When we write copy for our listings
- ☐ When we write copy for marketing our listings
- ☐ When we market our listings
- ☐ When we are working with buyers and working on solutions for them
- ☐ When we are navigating through the world of finance to help our clients
- ☐ When we are marketing ourselves to the outer universe
- ☐ When we are planning our days, weeks, months
- ☐ When we market ourselves on Social Media
- ☐ When we focus on planting seeds for future business

We have so many opportunities to flex those creative muscles in real estate. Why is this so important? I believe that human beings were made to be creative. I believe that we were made to think outside of the box. Look at nature. Are there any straight lines? Are there any boxes?

We go through life under systems that are always trying to put us in a box. That box becomes our identity. We, as humans, are always looking for a prescription for a problem or an ailment of some sort. I talk a lot about asking the right questions. Ask questions that cause your brain to go to different places and come up with alternative, more empowering solutions. Ask questions that get you to an answer. Instead of asking "Why ME?" for example, try asking "How Can I?" That question gets your creative subconscious mind working on the solution. Your mind is so, so, powerful when activated by the right thought patterns.

Thinks of a Chicken that lives in a pen. It accepts the scraps that are thrown in the pen. Its eyes are looking downward looking for scraps to eat. Its wings flap. If it gets startled it will flap vigorously and get a little lift off, in extreme circumstances, but it cannot fly out of the pen. Its wings are not strong enough to lift its body. Alternatively, look at an Eagle. It is larger than a chicken. It is heavier than a Chicken but its wings can take it wherever it wants to go. It is not satisfied with the scraps. It goes out and gets its own food. Think of the power of creativity, as your wings. Is it limited? Like the wings of a Chicken or can your ability to be creative enable you to discover new places, new opportunities, new ideas and new clients to help. Learn how to ask the right empowering questions to engage your creative wings and see what happens.

What do you want to be? A chicken in a pen or an eagle flying in the sky? Once you activate the creative part of your brain, it will take you to places that you didn't even know existed.

2. **Different Facets in Real Estate Fit Different Personality Types**

Drive around your community and begin to see opportunity everywhere. Introduce yourself to your City, or Town all over again. Just get in your car and go to places that you haven't explored before. Sometimes, we get caught up in our own routines, and our own habitual patterns. Do you notice that you tend to drive the same way to get to a certain destination? I took notice of this one day and made a decision to change my routes when I had a little more time to get somewhere. I would turn into subdivisions that I hadn't driven to for a while, or I would make a point of driving through an industrial area, and while I am driving, I am thinking about opportunity. I would drive to where I notice new subdivisions being developed and then figure out if there is some opportunity there. Maybe I could meet a builder. Maybe I already know of a builder and it might be a good idea for him to buy a lot to sell a home. Sometimes, I would be driving in a neighborhood that I hadn't visited for some time, and I would run across a "For Sale By Owner" sign, or I would discover a new park or a learn about some new rezoning applications, that are in process. These are opportunities. The world of Real Estate carries, boundless opportunities. There is business, for you to discover, everywhere in your community. There is much to learn. Think about all of the different ways that income can be earned with your Real Estate license and figure out the areas that have the most opportunity, or where there is untapped potential and begin to learn about that specific genre and see where it takes you.

There are so many facets of real estate to work in. There are so many different types of people to help, so many amazing opportunities to embrace. Even mini-niches can serve as the foundation of a whole business in real estate. There are no limits. Any one of you can build a great business, with any number of different client types you can gravitate to as you re-discover your own community. Open your mind and you will begin to see that there are boundless opportunities to earn commissions.

Here are just some:

1. Residential Homes in Neighborhoods
2. Working Farms and Large Acreages
3. Condos – Townhomes – Duplexes – Row Homes
4. Land for various Residential Developments
5. Commercial Land for Development
6. Income Producing properties
7. Leasing and Rental Management
8. Fractional Interests like Timeshare sales
9. Vacation Homes and Rentals
10. Hotel Sales
11. Industrial Land and Development
12. Investment Homes and Rental Properties
13. Project Marketing

14. New Construction working for Builders and Developers
15. Luxury Properties Concierge Type Services

These are just 15 different types of real estate business that can build a profitable business from. A number of the above compliment other facets as well, so there may be 5 or 10 of the above that you may dabble in as opportunities present themselves. That is exciting. Have you thought about that? Some of these offshoots will require more education, but that, too, will be available to you. The real estate profession can mean so many different things. Sometimes, your clients' needs lead you to other unexplored areas on real estate. That is amazing! Find me another line of work that offers that!

3. **Low Barrier to Enter Into the Profession**

We have the opportunity to earn incredible incomes in this business. What are we taught in childhood? Go to school, get a degree, and then get a good job. Even as the world changes, it is this mindset that is bred into us. Colleges and universities are full of students who will find a career with an income and be able to support a family. But not all of us have that opportunity. Post-secondary education costs money, a lot of money. Tens of thousands and, sometimes, hundreds of thousands of dollars are spent just to get a diploma. Billions of dollars are going to those institutions every year.

But you can order up a real estate course for under $1,000, in most cases, and take that course while still working in your J-O-B and getting licensed. There are a few follow-up courses in a lot of jurisdictions and then you are rocking and rolling in the real estate business.

There is no screening process. There are few offices or brokerages that will refuse to have you join their team. Pay your membership dues to the various support organizations and you are on your way for under $3,000 in most cases and, sometimes, for even less.

Now that you are in business, two things will happen. I see it all the time. The low barrier of entry will either help you, or it will hinder you.

"You may only succeed if you desire succeeding; you may only fail if you do not mind failing."
~Philippos

What this means is, you will either think of the low barrier as a low risk, minimal impact, route to failure and insignificance, or...

You will treat it as an enormous GIFT and do everything you can to maximize the impact of it.

The fact that you are here, reading this copy of *Attract* tells me that you are looking for the latter. Good for you... you are in the right place! I was bankrupt when I began my real estate career. My wife and I shared a car. We were renting a basement suite. I started as an assistant for my friend; the company he was associated with paid for the real estate licensing course on my behalf. That is how I was introduced to the Real Estate business. Someone else paid for the course. I did invest a little bit of my own money. I had to save my money to pay to become licensed, and pay for the fees associated with that and I had to use Nicole's credit card to pay for the "Errors and Omissions Insurance" that is required to be licensed. I had no idea what I was getting into. I had no clear understanding about Buying and Selling Real Estate. No personal experience to draw upon. I just fell into the business because my friend needed some help and the doors were opened for me. I could have had the attitude that I spoke about earlier in this book. I could have - well – I believe, I did have that attitude – "I'll just give IT a shot and see if IT works out." Luckily, I moved past that made a clear decision to turn this opportunity into a Lifetime career and build a wonderful life for my family. I am so thankful for the people that introduced me to the Real Estate business today. I had no idea the GIFT that was given to me. The magnitude of that gift was not revealed to me until yea er. I hope you adopt this view and appreciate that th barrier to enter" into the real estate business as a career is an amazing gift and you are going to make the most of that gift.

Okay. What else makes real estate a GREAT Business?

4. **No Stock – No Receivables – No Shipping – No Storefront**

Let's compare You INC., as a "REALTOR®-Preneur" and your business to what most entrepreneurs are faced with. The fact that they are selling something: a service, a widget, a physical product. Logistics are involved. There are a lot of businesses that give terms on payment. You have to get the product to the customer or consumer somehow. Sometimes, there has to be a place that the customer can visit. Stocking products, warehousing, trucking: There are jobs to be filled and people to hire. Now you are subject to employment standards and have to remit money to the government. Hiring and firing is not fun. Training. Shipping. Manufacturing. Ever-changing markets and trends. Importing and exporting. Paying leases and searching out locations. Expansion and scaling your business. Marketing expenses. Working with investors. Government regulations impacting imports and exports. Obtaining Parts...

There are so many challenges that entrepreneurs face, but let's look at what the "REALTOR®-PRENEUR" has to face:

He/She gets up in the morning, looks in the mirror and says, ***"What are you going to do today? What are you going to accomplish today to move the ball down the field? Where are you going to create opportunities for the business?"***

You can work from home. You can work from a coffee shop. You can work at your space in your brokerage office.

Other than your inventory of listings, you have nothing to stock.

There are no receivables...you get paid out of proceeds of a transaction. The Brokerage and the Conveyancers control the money. Your commissions are always protected.

Now that online signing programs are possible for contracts, you can save a lot of vehicle wear and tear. I now drive about 40,000 km less a year than I did in the beginning of my career!

There is no storefront. YOU are the storefront. It's just you, your cell phone/tablet/laptop, your satchel/purse/brief case and your website. Real estate

is the most cost-effective business out there if you build it properly. If you employ the 4X Formula and master all four facets—Attract, Attain, Serve and Retain—it will get easier and more cost-effective as you progress.

Soon you begin scaling, adding staff and new processes; you start growing exponentially, but the risk is low. Because, at that point, you are simply leveraging time...that's all. When you begin to increase your $/hour, then your time becomes a major asset of your business. If you build it right, your time value should grow exponentially.

And that brings us to the fifth reason to be in real estate:

5. **No Ceiling on Income Earning Potential**

There is literally no limit to your income earning potential. None. There is no basement either. But you are not a chicken in a pen; you are an eagle that wants to soar to new heights...right?

We utilize the 4X Formula, a business model I discovered after banging my head against the wall for 17 years. It took losing everything, giving it all away and hitting rock bottom to get to the point of clarity that has caused me to start this revolution.

But with all of this in mind, during those years, I always felt that there was amazing opportunity to harness, a lot of money to make. Eventually, I *did* make a lot of money. Once you understand your potential and your brain has been stretched, there is no stopping you. Did I experience doubts once in a while? Did I experience fear? Did I worry about paying the bills sometimes? YES. Yes, I did. But my brain had been stretched and, once that happens, you can't go backwards.

This is where we are going, people. We are going forward. We are taking steps in a positive direction every single day. For those of you who are already members of the 4XFormula Quick Commission Accelerator Course, this is it. The minute you hit the button and got into the Members Area of this course, you literally drew a line in the sand and stepped over it. Every step you take will be in a positive direction and, suddenly, you will feel your mind stretching and stretching, expanding your image of who you can become and what you can accomplish! It is a beautiful thing.

You will learn to 4X all parts of your business. You will maximize your earning potential for your time output. You will maximize and fertilize the seed planting of your business. You will be depositing multiple cheques every single month and your annual goal will become monthly goals.

Yes...I said it. If you want it, you can have it. I remember when all I wanted to make was $100,000 in commissions for the year; but now I have earned more than that in commission cheques many times in one month! You can, too. I know this, because I am not special. I am just a regular guy, who lives in a regular town with a population of less than 100,000 people and I came from nothing. I was a poor farm boy who thought success was working in a grocery store making $20/hour!! I make over 10 times that now! Do you think I can go backwards? No way. It is impossible.

I want that for you.

Believe

Okay. Have we increased your level of belief a little? A lot? This is the mindset that you will need to absorb as we go through this. Believe in yourself and your abilities. We will get you there.

We just spent some time talking about why the real estate business is great. This is really important because you need to know that you are in the right vehicle. You are in the Tesla. It's a great vehicle. It's efficient and cost-effective to run. But first we have to put the tires on.

Now that you have a concrete belief that you are in the right business, what are the mindsets that we need to cultivate to build our belief in our own abilities to succeed in this business?

"A real entrepreneur is somebody who has no safety net underneath them."~Henry Kravis

Close the Back Door. Decide to Succeed.

Life is made up of a series of decisions. One decision after another. That's it.

"I'll see if it works out" or *"I'll give it a shot for 24 months and see if it is the business for me"*; those are not the approaches to take. Failure is not an option. Take that option off the table. You are here because you want to succeed, and you will accept nothing else. There is no other option. Lock all the doors. Burn all the bridges. Commit to what you have written down.

Once you have established and fleshed out your WHY and written your goals down and have made a mental commitment then you know what you need to be focusing on. Nothing else. Challenges? Oh, yes...they will come. But there is no other option...there is no other way...you face it head on and figure out how to get over, under, around, or through that challenge. You learn from it and then move on. When you fall, *fall forward*, so when you get up you are little b ahead. Because you will get up. Failure is not an option.

Sorry about that. I didn't mean to get all "motivational". But I am passionate about this. This is the truth. This is the most important of all the mindsets that need to fill your brain. Are you INTERESTED? Being "interested" in success will not get your there. You must be absolutely committed to success and you will get there. Are you COMMITTED?

Your Biggest Asset is the Power of Your Mind

You have to guard your mind as if your life depends on it. Because it does. It is the one factor that will be responsible for either your success or your failure. That is it. *You, Incorporated,* remember? You, INC.

So how do you do that?

- ☐ Focus on what you want, not what you fear.
- ☐ Focus on your own growth and forget about small thinkers. They have no power over you.
- ☐ Focus on your own goals and why you want to achieve them.
- ☐ Focus on what it will be like to achieve those goals.
- ☐ Focus on the celebration of achievement and what that would feel like.
- ☐ Focus on what you can control.
- ☐ Focus on doing, on being present, on being in the moment
- ☐ Focus on serving others well.
- ☐ Focus on becoming your best version of yourself.
- ☐ Focus on getting out of survive mode and into *THRIVE mode.*
- ☐ Focus on your loved ones when you are with them. They will recharge you

☐ Focus on creating a positive impression wherever you go and with whoever you run into.

Focus like this, and you will be unstoppable! **You will smash through your goals**!

I know it with absolute certainty.

Here's a quote from Napoleon Hill, the author of the book ***"Think and Grow Rich."***

(Notice that the title of the book is ***THINK** and Grow Rich*? Not *Hope and Grow Rich*, not *Complain and Grow Rich*, not *Fail and Grow Rich*, not *Listen to what Other People Say about You and Grow Rich,* not *Succumb to Challenges and Grow Rich,* and not *Speak and Grow Rich).*

THINK. It all starts in the mind.

Remember earlier we touched on this quote. Never forget this quote. Your mind MUST have complete BELIEF. Its ok if you are not there 100% right now. Remember to refer to your "Why Worksheet" and your "Goals" multiple times per day.

"Whatever the Mind of Man Can Conceive and Believe, he will Achieve."

—Napoleon Hill

QUICK COMMISSION BLUEPRINT

I have inserted the "Quick Commission Blueprint" into this book so that we cover everything for you. Some of you may have already downloaded the Quick Commission Blueprint as an e-Book and may be already in possession of this information, but I thought it would be important to have it here for everyone who receives this book. I do touch on some things that we discuss in this book, within the Quick Commission Blueprint, so I apologize if you find those concepts repetitive, but this "book within a book", is really the foundation to the concepts that we apply in further chapters and that will become clear as you get deeper into this book. If you have already read the Quick Commission Blueprint, then you can skip this chapter if you like. It's up to you. If perhaps, you need a reminder, then carry on.

A Proven 30-Day Strategy to Set Up Your $100k/year Real Estate Business

The *Quick Commission Blueprint* is based on a simple formula; its concepts are uncomplicated and straightforward. Anyone can do the action steps. You don't have to have special sales abilities or a certain personality type to be successful in the real estate business. In this book, I'm going to show you how you can set up your real estate business for massive success following some basic principles.

I want you to feel incredibly secure in your real estate business. I want you to feel in control and secure in the knowledge that you too can have commission checks coming in consistently, month after month.

If you are finding your business is slow, or you have busy spurts, but the end result is not a lot of profit, and you're realizing that you are not far from having real financial issues, you know you must change what you are doing ... or how you are doing it. Perhaps your situation begins to stir fear within you. Insecurity is not a good feeling. I remember that situation; none of us are immune. My goal is to get you free from "surviving" and into "thriving."

In order to teach you how to set up a successful real estate business in 30 days, let's imagine I am brand new at this. Let's go a step further and imagine that am starting from scratch with no contacts. Let's imagine that I take an airplane from California and head east. I have enough money to pay for food and a place to stay for up to four months, and I have a little money to use to begin my real estate business. Imagine that I jump from the plane and parachute into a new town where I do not know anyone. I have no history, no family members, nothing else that relates to my past. I land right next to a real estate office, walk in, and begin my real estate career. I am totally alone. I know no one. I have zero connections.

The information that follows will illustrate the exact steps to take to set up a successful real estate business in as little as 30 days.

If I were to look at what other coaches are doing, they typically give these 5 pieces of advice:

1. Call all the FSBO's (For Sale by Owners) that you can find and get an appointment

2. Call all of the expired listings you can find and get an appointment
3. Do an open house; meet buyers
4. Spend money on Facebook ads and put effort into other online marketing/website creation, etc.
5. Ask for business from your sphere of influence: friends, family, and connections.

While all of these are good activities, if they are not done correctly, they will NOT work and can do more harm than good.

There are four crucially important activities upon which I would embark *before* doing any one of these activities. Essentially, I want to stack the deck in my favor; I want to play to win.

If I am to invest my energy, money, and time (EMT), I want as much leverage as I can get. In your situation, do you want to stack the cards in your favor to provide you the best chance of success?

Here are two issues I have made it my mission to abolish:

1. "REALTOR® Poverty" – only the top 10% make more than $90,000 a year. The average income is $40,000. The average person's salary of all "working people" in the USA is approximately $60,000, which is $20,000 more than that of the average Real Estate agent. We need to fix this ... and rapidly!
2. Lack of "REALTOR Respectability" – Real Estate professionals consistently fall in the Top 10 LEAST TRUSTED professionals every year! This is a horrible situation. We need to change this image to become part of the MOST TRUSTED professionals.

Cause and Effect

If 90% of Real Estate professionals are in Survival Mode all the time, then it sets them up to make bad decisions. There are more than one million Real Estate agents who are operating as "Prisoners of Hope," and then they are out of business in 2-3 years. According to the National Association of REALTORS®, only about 13% will make it. Those who enjoy the fruits of the business will finally begin to experience success after 15-16 years. I definitely do not want you to have to wait that long to create a successful business.

The 4 Steps of Preparation

My goal is to get you armed, create ways for you to win, and sharpen your skills to gain the advantage. This has become my defining purpose – this is my life mission.

Four tasks need to be accomplished before you start. I am going to help you set up a plan for success. Before developing a plan, you need information. To execute the plan, you need the skills to ensure successful conversions. Eventually, your EMT quotient will grow.

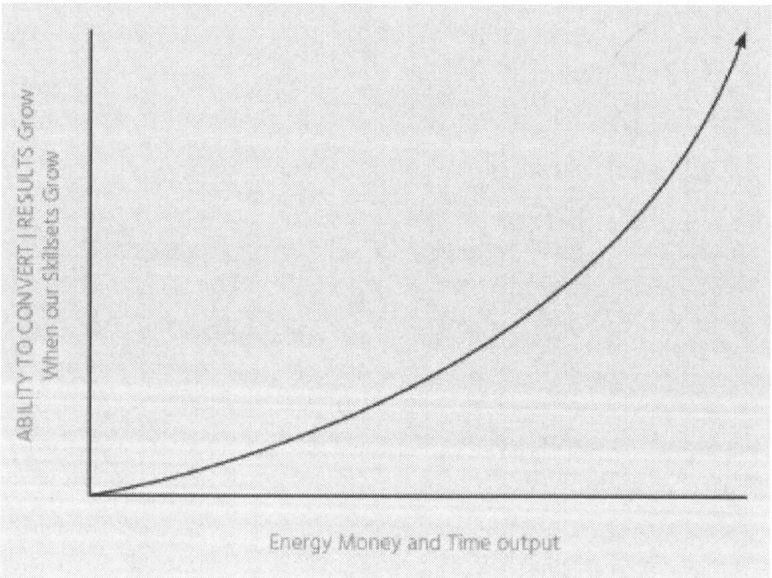

This approach is not any sort of magic pill for your success but, at the same time, I believe this is critical to your success. There is no one else teaching this approach, designed for you to learn properly to execute and create better conversions. For that, you need to work on, and eventually master, the skills required in order to implement these principals and increase your profit. That is why I developed the 4X Formula Quick Commission Accelerator Program. For New Agents who see the value in getting proper training to shorten their time frame to success, this course is transformative. (I hope you take a moment at the end of the book to learn how to enroll.) However, the information in the Quick Commission Blueprint will give you the ability to set your targets and determine how to make money quickly.

Define Your Goals

What actually is your goal? Besides making over $100,000 this year in real estate, your plan is to attract business, attract opportunities, and attract buyers and sellers who want to do business with you NOW, SOON, or LATER.

I want you to approach this strategy as if this is your first day as a licensed Real Estate agent. Get rid of all your preconceived notions and just stick to the following with commitment. Ready? Here we go!

#1 Identify Your Target Market

PRICE POINT

What is the most popular price range? What is producing 40% of the sales in your market area? At what price point are 40% of the sales occurring? These are the listings you want to attract. We'll come back to this in a minute.

PRODUCT TYPE

Once you have settled on the most popular price point, you want to determine the product type that best fits that price point. That is, what home type represents the most sales? Is it detached, bungalow style homes? Is it condos? Is it 3-bedroom townhouses?

Understanding the price point and the specific type of home will help you focus your efforts on the right things. My experience is that when you do that, the opportunities seem to present themselves. Know exactly where you want to focus because there will be the product you want to list for sale, market for sale, and sell to others. It will have the greatest volume of business for you. Your chances of creating more business from the business that fits your price point are exponentially greater and will provide you a higher chance of more quickly producing positive results. You must focus on this.

BUYER TYPE

What are the characteristics of buyers who are interested in the product and price point? Who are they? What is their average income level? Where do they hang out? What is their marital status? Are they young families or are they empty nesters? Are they employed locally, or do they commute to work? What attributes of the product type are most appealing to this by type? What about location and neighborhood style? What are the drivers for decision marking? Is there a concern for affordability? ... Leverage? ... Downsizing? ... Upsizing? ... Future potential? ... Short-term or long-term planning? ... Location? ... Schools? ... Sports? ... Opportunities for children? ... Career opportunities? ... Close to shopping? ... Busy or laid-back lifestyle? Ask a lot of questions to understand the buyer type. The answer just well may be a combination of many things. You therefore must be in a constant mode of seeking to understand what drives decisions for this type of buyer.

The Power of Focus and why this is so important

Once you start to drill down on what you want, you begin to visualize an avatar of the buyer. You then begin to picture features of the home, its style and type, you begin to unleash your power of **focus**.

There is a phenomenon called **FREQUENCY ILLUSION**. Have you ever heard of it? Here is an example: I recently took a trip to the UK and then on to Barcelona, Spain. For some reason, my wife started noticing “fanny packs.” In the UK they are referred to as “bum bags” because the word “fanny” refers to something else and is somewhat frowned upon. So, we will refer to them as “bum bags” for now. Once she decided to focus on them, she saw them everywhere. Suddenly, to my shock and amazement, things changed. I went from never speaking about, or even noticing, these “bum bags” to seeing them everywhere. It became kind of a funny joke. Suddenly our brains were keyed into noticing 2 to 4 people in every 10 were wearing one. Have you ever bought a car and then all of a sudden saw that type of car everywhere? That happens to me every time and this is FREQUENCY ILLUSION.

How do we use this to our advantage? Frequency Illusion is related to business and motivation, and business planning, because you can’t be motivated to do something about which you aren’t aware. If you never consciously think about something, then it’s impossible to do anything about it. The normality that we are fighting against is simply operating on autopilot. You spend much more of your life on autopilot than you realize. Your conscious mind is quite powerful, but your subconscious mind is a million times more powerful. When you focus on certain things, you begin to notice the opportunities. You create a more defined keenness to that subject matter. It’s like a hyper focus. So, to put this to work for you, you need to tell your brain on what to focus – consciously at first.

That is why we go through the foundations stage of the 4X Formula Real Estate Mastery before the applicable tactics and strategies and how-to’s because it is important to train your brain to focus on what you want to go after. We define and crystalize it so that you start to train your brain to figure out how to get it.

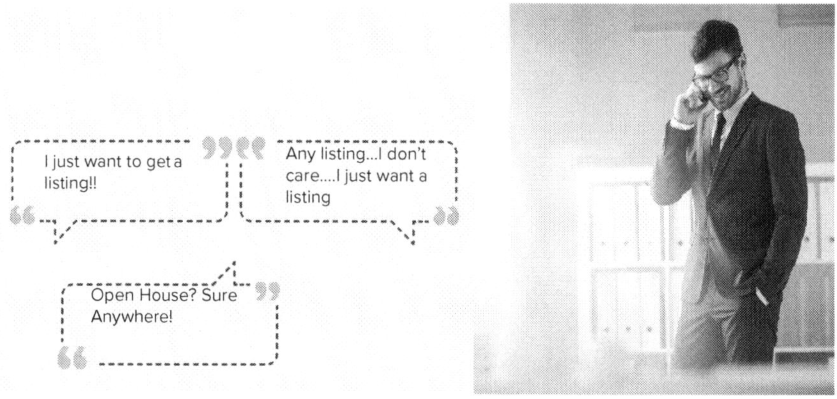

Here is just another application of that. Here are examples of the self-talk of most agents when they first get into the Real Estate business:

I was the same way. I did not care and just wanted inventory. I wanted a bunch of listings, or any listing. I just wanted something in which to put my energy.

Are you able to relate to that? It's not a bad mentality. Actually, it is to be commended, but let's not get confused. I don't want you to eliminate the other types of business if it comes to you. I still take listings outside of my business plan. I still list unique properties that are in price points where fewer people are buying. I am not proposing that you should necessarily turn away listings. However, there are times that you need to set the terms and standards. I don't want you to push business away or refuse business that is outside of your plan but be careful where you commit your resources. Remember your EMT. You only have so much; be aware.

Our purpose is first to figure out the easiest and most satisfying "prey." Focusing on listings ... getting listings ... any listing ... a listing of some sort ... anywhere... is NOT good enough.

This is not good enough because it is not defined enough. If that is your goal, then you will take horrible listings and cause yourself to be subject to the Seller defining your business plan for selling that listing. You become the prey. What do I mean by that? You must decide whether you want to be a chicken in a coop or an eagle. Have you ever heard of the term "eagle eye"? The eyesight of the eagle is among the strongest in the animal kingdom, with an eyesight estimated at 4 to 8 times stronger than that of the average human. An eagle is said to be able to spot a rabbit 3 miles away!! It is a predator. It fixates on its prey and goes after it. It flies around and knows exactly what it is seeking. When it decides it is time to go after the prey, the eagle moves very quickly and expertly and decisively. A chicken walks around, pecking at whatever it steps on and whatever falls on the ground around them ... the scraps. Humans have to put covers over their chicken coops because chickens are so unaware of predators that they will not defend themselves properly. Chickens can't imagine getting out of that pen. Chickens rely on the scraps that the farmer throws into their pen. There are a lot of agents operating like chickens right now. But not you. You are an eagle. You know how to hunt for the best prey. You know where to establish your nest so that you are as close to the prey that you want. That is your zone. You define your hunting grounds. You don't rely on anyone throwing you the scraps. See the difference? You are either part of the 80% of agents fighting for the scraps like a chicken or you are an eagle in the top 20% who is securing 80% of the business.

ACTIVATE Frequency Illusion

To put this to work for you, it is paramount to figure out the segment of the market that is best for your focus. Next, determine the buyer's characteristics. What stage in life are they? What is the challenge they are facing with which they need help? Start to think about who that buyer is and what is the focus. This will create opportunities for you.

Here's an example. If 40% of the sales in your area are in the $450,000 to $500,000 range, then determine what is the most popular product or type that is selling at that price point. Who are the people buying those properties? What are the aspects of that property type that make it popular? What are the aspects of the surrounding neighborhoods? What are the aspects of the nearby amenities? Why is it popular? How does financing affect the purchase process of this product type? How does financing affect this buyer type? Understanding the nuances of the specific type of financing can help you in your conversations with the target market.

#2 Mortgage Broker Meetings

Schedule to take two local Mortgage Specialists out for lunch. Mortgage Brokers are about to become your ally. Nurture them for business and try to get a buyer lead from them. This should become a habit with every person with whom you spend time in a business-friendly way. This is an opportunity to build a relationship and create a strategic alliance. If you feel that you can complement each other's businesses and you truly enjoy each other's company, I would say that is a very successful meeting/lunch. Try to make this a regular occurrence to keep top of mind with this professional. Some of your best marketing dollars are spent on lunches like this. Not only can you potentially get referrals from this mortgage broker, but you could also refer clients to them.

Your main focus for this first meeting, other than relationship building, is to ask questions that will help you learn about the most common mortgage product types that most commonly fits with the Buyer type. Get a clear understanding of how that mortgage works. Learn the details for which the lender is looking and how someone will qualify. This will also give you more insight into the characteristics of this Buyer type. Get clear on the mortgage rates and how to calculate payments to fit the budget of your buyer. This will help you in your later conversations. Also, it is good to talk about protocol and systems. Ask them how they like to operate. Ask them to walk you through a typical process with a client. Thus, when you are talking to your new clients and planning to refer this Mortgage Broker, you will inform them appropriately and prepare them for what's in store for them and how the process works. People take a lot of comfort in good preparation. When you set expectations properly, you bring a sense of calmness to the process for the people you serve. This is how you win people to your business circle and create consistent, ongoing business.

You are gaining more clarity on the subject of your focus. Frequency Illusion is starting to take shape. You will meet people who fit this category because you are focusing on it now. You need other professionals on your side to help process things efficiently, and, at the same time, create a strategic alliance that will be part of your business building team. Mortgage Lenders/Brokers are the first alliance that you need to make. You commit to referring business to this new contact and focus on doing that as fast as you can. With your new laser focus, it will happen.

#3 Become a Master Specialist

Absorb everything about this market product. Study the data. Get to know all of the listings, know the product. Look them up in your MLS system, book appointments, and go out and preview all of those homes that are currently listed. Become a specialist in that price point and the product type. Saturate your brain with this market. Learn all of the advantages and disadvantages, and the little nuances, and differences that you can talk about. Notice all of the characteristics about every listing that fits within that product type and price point. Arm yourself with knowledge about that product type in every way so you can have great conversations with people when the time comes. This is your business. Every day. Learn something new about this target market and this product type. Be the first person to see a listing when it hits the MLS. Your business card will be on the counter first every time. There is nothing else that is more important. Go to view a minimum of 5 per day at first until you have a good understanding of the current inventory. This takes time and it takes dedication. If you want to build a successful real estate business, you have to be willing to do the groundwork.

#4 Market the Product

Now we begin the process of marketing. You have spent time preparing, focusing and filling your brain with input from many sources. This is considered black and white data. Make notes on what you discover. You have had lunch meetings and are learning things through listening. You have been walking through all of the products, as well as looking at the pictures and tours online. In a very short time, you will be the absolute master in this Target Market. It will happen very quickly. Another really neat thing will happen: Just the act of performing all of these activities will cause something to occur that will attract business to you. This happens to me all the time. The moment that you begin to focus hard on something, an opportunity arises, and sometimes it has nothing to do with what you are focusing on. This is another offshoot that happens. Embrace this and notice this. Keep tuned into this possibility.

Once you have determined the target product, the next action is to book an open house. If you are going to do an open house, then stack the cards in your favor. Your goal is to meet people. Meet as many people as you can who are interested in that type of product. Stir things up. Make your presence known. It has to be an event, an Extravaganza. It takes a lot of work, organization, and planning but it is worth it in the end. We are not able to go into this in great detail here but included in the Quick Commission Accelerator Course we have a 4-part series dedicated to The Open House Strategies which includes over 90 minutes of video and a combination of tools. We go over the details of preparation, the event day, and then we cover the 7 Stages of

Contact when you meet people in order to create a successful outcome every time. I encourage you to enroll to maximize the opportunities that can present themselves in The Open House. There is more information at the back of this book.

5 Typical Activities

Now let's look at the five typical activities that everyone teaches and see how we can implement those strategies within the parameters I have just explained.

#1 "Call All the FSBOs and Expired Listings you can find and get an appointment."

Now that you are armed with knowledge, you can determine which FSBO or Expired Listing you want to approach as long as they meet your target market criteria. You are not necessarily looking to go after all of the Expired and FSBO opportunities in your community. There are criteria they must satisfy, or it is a total waste of EMT. You are prepared and armed with a definite focus now. You know what price listings are selling for and you have been through every comparable home, so you can give some great insights to these people. Depending on the stats you read, roughly only 10% of the FSBOs out there actually succeed in selling on their own and it is usually because they sold to someone that they already knew. More often than not, it was not because of the owner's amazing marketing skills. A lot of FSBOs end up calling an Agent to help out eventually and you will be that person as long as you had a great meeting and kept in touch. Expired Listings represent a large portion of the "current" listings out there, as well. There is a percentage of the current inventory that will not sell. Never forget this fact. With that in mind, you will develop a systematic approach to create mindshare in the target market areas with those current listings so when they do expire, you will be top of mind with them. The Past Expires have to meet certain qualifications that you will impose based on your strategy. If they do, you want to be able to position yourself as the next best choice when they decide to enter the market again.

#2 "Do an Open House – Meet Buyers"

Virtual Open Houses

Screen Share videos utilizing a 3D Tour – live Open House Watch Parties on Facebook or YouTube. These are very effective and they live on in the virtual world. You get to show off your personality and it can be shared over and over. A lot of Listing Systems are allowing direct links to go into the main system for these events and you can promote that approach by utilizing very powerful online search engines. These can be done in addition to personally attended open houses, especially if Physical Distancing is still encouraged/required.

Open House Events

Open House Events are valuable for you to meet prospects face to face. Utilize the Open House Events, and all of the activities leading up to them, to create relationships, attract buyers, and attract future sellers in your direct target market zone. These efforts will pay off exponentially when performed with intention and creativity. On my YouTube Channel and the podcast (search for 4X Formula Real Estate training), you may have heard me talk about the 4 Levels of Client Types. The NOW – SOON – LATER – PAST clients all can be huge reservoirs of business. You may even meet some unicorns ... and that is fine. There are a lot of opportunities here. Simply scheduling an open house is not enough. There is a system to follow and it is a formula that works. That is the differentiator. Once you have drilled down to the target market and product, you want to focus your attention on your target market of Buyers that you want to attract. Then you can "speak their language" and communicate toward their "pain points" and their "pleasure points." If you do this right, you will pretty well guarantee meeting a minimum of 1 NOW Buyer from those efforts. Also, you will meet some SOON clients and FUTURE clients. All of these people attend open houses. You may be thinking to yourself: "What if I don't have any listings yet?" Excellent question. We will get to that in a bit.

#3 Spend money on Facebook Ads and put efforts in Online marketing/website creation

Now that you have a clear idea of the "What" and the "Who," you can create your marketing. Part of the reason that new Agents have a hard time gaining momentum is that they are not clear on WHO they want to serve and WHAT product they want to market. They focus on creating some sort of "brand" that they think is cool. Colors, photo style, logo, fonts are all what they think is attractive. But they have not spent any energy or time thinking about that target market of the business that they want to obtain. They use a "hit or miss" approach. Sometimes, by happenstance, it works, but more often than not it does not work. While they may create an attractive brand, it is only attracting a small percentage of their buyer/seller market. In some cases, it is repulsing or confusing their target market. Here's an example: If the average sale price is $400,000 to $550,000 and I decide that I want to create a brand that is focused on the luxury market, and only 1% of the sales over $1,000,000, then what I am effectively doing is working against the market. I am not attracting the right target market, am I? The risk is that the Avatar Character of the market that produces the largest number of sales is offended by that marketing. It may be repulsed by the colors or style or the "look" I am presenting. That becomes negative marketing. I am marketing to tell people NOT to do business with me. We don't want this to happen.

This is why taking the time to 1) determine the price point of the majority of sales, and 2) determine the product type, and 3) clarify the buyer type is so important. It influences all aspects of the style of your marketing. Here are a few things to consider:

- ☐ What font should you use?
- ☐ What colors speak to this target market?
- ☐ What is the best Imagery for your marketing?
- ☐ The pictures of yourself: What is your posture and how should you be dressed?
- ☐ The marketing messaging.
- ☐ The communication style that your target market prefers

Take a look at the following images. Which one of these appeals or relates to you? Do you notice yourself gravitating to one of these images?

This expands into everything that you do, every marketing element:

- What do your business cards look like?
- Think about the style of your website.
- What dominant colors do you use?
- Everything is intentional.

- Should your clothing blend into those colors well?
    - Are they fresh?
    - Are they warm?
    - Is it business casual?
    - Is it a business dress, power suit style?
- Should you have a picture of you and your family?
    - Is it a full-length shot or torso or headshot or action oriented?
    - Should you have many types of pictures showing up on each page of the site?
- What is the housing type that Is in the background picture on your website...or what type of interi-or shot should be used?

These questions will be much easier to answer when you have taken the time to define your Avatar.

Your Facebook Page profile should match your site, and the things you talk about on your Facebook page all speak to your target audience. The product type that you feature on your Facebook page and your website are speaking to attract this Avatar that you have created. If your target market product type is Attached Town Homes that are over 1,500 square feet and have a minimum of 3 bedrooms priced between $375,000 and $500,000, then do not have images of city backgrounds and condo buildings showing the views off of the awesome balcony looking at the ocean. Your target market does not relate to this. Keep it consistent.

#4 Designing Facebook/Instagram Ads to Promote an Open House directly to your target market

Targeted Boost Ads are much more economical than any other type of advertising, and extremely effective. The power of Facebook is mind-blowing. You can figure out where most of these people are living, understand their interests and hobbies, target age group, as well as target what they may be discussing with their friends on Facebook This will help you get those ads to show up in front of them in their feed. A $20 Boosted Promotion for an Open House will get it in front of a lot of targeted people if you set it up correctly. However, if you don't understand who the buyer is, then you will miss the mark and waste a lot of money.

And now the final Action Item:

#5 Ask for Business from your Sphere of Influence – friends, family, and connections

You may have heard this before: "Don't be a secret agent."

You have family and/or friends who live in your local area. You have a past, a history of some sort. You may have lived where you are for your whole life. So, you have connections who go as far back as elementary school and the sports teams that you were part of. If you were involved in dance or gymnastics or certain clubs and organizations as you were growing up, you would have made some strong connections. Any jobs in the past will have created some relationships. You have a circle of influence. You know a lot of people. This is the first thing that you should do: begin to develop your Circle of Influence or Sphere of Influence list of names and contacts. You know a lot more people than you realize. Take the time consciously organize these contacts onto a list. This list should be alive and growing and transforming all the time. Most importantly, this list is meant to grow. This is the beginning of your database.

I hate to be the bearer of bad news, but this is going to be where you get the least business. If you have been very busy lately due to your "connections" and have not taken any time to do the above-mentioned activities to grow your list, then you will run out of leads or your business will not continue to build and grow. In my course, I refer to the Circle of Influence as a dot. Previously, we were calculating all the people you ran into in your life on a regular basis. The soccer coach, the barista at Starbucks, the woman at the drug store. You are the real estate agent who connects all those people with your Circle of Influence.

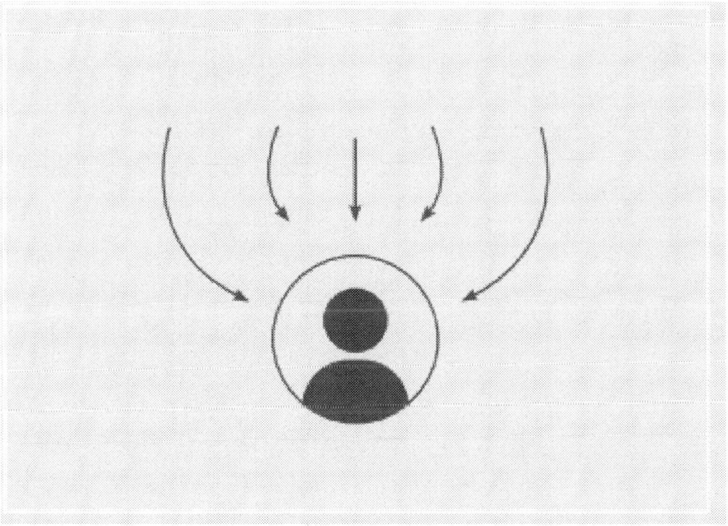

The goal is to not to expand your dot...not to make yourself *bigger*. That may be your instinct; that may have been what you were taught. But try to think of your goal differently. You want to connect a lot of dots, to enter into other people's worlds, and then become a positive influence in their lives. Then their dot, which is connected to other dots, will begin a gravitational pull to you. That is the best, most fruitful and least expensive way to grow your business. This is how you create a business of never-ending referrals. Do not rely on your dot, but at the same time "don't be a secret agent." I call it a dot instead of a circle because if you look at the stars in the sky, they look like dots. Each one seems so insignificant compared to the universe. That is how you need to view yourself. There are a lot of people who believe that their little world of connections is bigger than it really is. If someone continues to think that way, they will not experience the richness in meeting and connecting with a lot of other people, or dots. They will be so consumed with expanding "their circle" and "what is inside their circle" that they won't get outside of their circle. See the difference between a circle and a dot? Connecting dots can take you to many places and is ever expanding. The truth is, in your current circle, there is business there for sure, but it is unwise and very limiting to believe that your little world of connections is going to feed you all the business that you will need to expand and eventually build your dream business.

I think that you will agree that these 5 items are important activities, but you need to be intentional and create an appropriate plan. Activate and employ the 4 Steps of Preparation and it will make all the difference in the world when you go to work on those 5 action steps. The truth is, there are many ways to build your real estate business that are not mentioned here. Depending on your target market, once you have taken on the Four Steps of Preparation, other avenues for attracting business will be woven into your regular business building activities. The Four Steps of Preparation are what opens the door. They are the blueprint for experiencing success quickly in the Real Estate business. Think like an eagle ... not like a chicken.

Now back to our scenario where I have to start from scratch in a new city. Remember that #5 will not apply to me because I have zero connections. None. So, I have to rely upon the first 4 strategies. I have parachuted into some unknown town and started my Real Estate career. The question that was posed was, "What would I do?"

I would do all of those things that I just noted. Now armed with knowledge and understanding, and having identified my prey, I know what I want to go after. I know where I will have the best success. I have started creating strategic alliances. I understand the characteristics of the product and I understand the attributes and traits of the Buyers and Sellers of this product. At the very minimum, I have at least thought about it more deeply than has my competition, in most cases. I am prepared for when the time comes to get into a conversation with my target market; I can come across as an authority. I can show more empathy. I have more clarity about their needs. I know all of the product out there right now, intimately. If I am challenged, I am armed with the knowledge to gently counter, or explain, or educate, in a respectful way.

Here is an example. You are doing an open house. A buyer enters. He/she looks around and you are having surface discussions at this point. Before getting into a deeper discussion, he says to you, “Well this is overpriced!” Instead of being offended or being taken back with that firm and confident statement, you now are armed with knowledge and you have seen the products out there that are comparable. You have an answer for that statement. There are so many different ways to answer this and I am not offering a “script,” here but let’s explore some answers that can come out of it, depending on the research that you have done.

You could say, “Oh well, I have seen every home in this price point, and I agree it is maybe priced a little aggressively, but not too badly. Perhaps the seller will be open to an offer. I am not sure. But I did view a couple of homes 2 blocks away that I thought were really good deals and they both had bigger yards...” Take an objection and create an opportunity out of it. Figure out how to serve and be of help. Help the Buyer get to the intended objective.

Ask if he/she is working with an agent and, if not, offer to book some showings to research the product to help make a great buying decision. This is how you lock people in.

Or, you may say, “You know, I toured about 4 or 5 homes in this price point over the last week or so and, actually, if you take into account the large yard, the RV parking, and the fact that it backs up on the park, I think that this is a good deal. But you shouldn’t just take my word for it. This is a really good neighborhood. Would you like to take a look at a few other homes to help you get an idea of value and to see what is out there for the money? What is the price point at which you are most comfortable?"

You cannot tackle those types of statements if you don't have market knowledge. This is why this is so important. It shows that you are a professional. If over 40% of the sales are in this price range, and if you are doing an open house in this price point, and you have marketed it well, then you will have good attendance because that is where 40% of the buyers are. And, if you have studied that market and gained an understanding of that buyer and have spoken to a mortgage professional to gain clarity on the nuances of financing for this target market, you now have all the material you need to speak to people intelligently and find ways to help them make a great decision. This is "WARM" business. These are people that are walking through the door who have no idea how awesome you are going to be for them. They were not prepared for this. They did not expect this. But here you are, ready for the opportunity. You only need 1 person or family or couple or whatever per open house — only 1. Shoot for 2, but ensure you attract 1. Then you will make $100,000 or more per year!

What Do You Do If You Don't have Any Listings?

Here are a few tips for now. Work on these and something will happen. You will get opportunities if you focus on the following:

Set up numerous open houses to meet buyers, but do not do it haphazardly. The senior agent who has an overpriced listing in the middle of nowhere and a product type that only 2% of the market is buying, is not where I would want to do an open house. But this is what happens! The Senior Agent will give the new agents the "pain in the butt" listings to do open houses at to appease their sellers. Watch out for this! This is why we have to prepare in advance. Do these 5 things below and within 30 days you will be doing open

OPEN Houses

houses every weekend and locking in buyers and nu opportunities for listings. Here are some suggestions

1. Find an agent in your office who has a product th that market.
2. Find another agent in another office who has a product that fits that market.
3. Find an FSBO and ask to market their home for FREE. If you find the buyer, you will only charge the Buyer side of commission – don't even ask for the listing yet.
4. Find an Expired Listing – do the same as #3 – don't even ask for the listing yet.
5. Do as many open houses as you possibly can. Book 2 per Saturday and 2 per Sunday every weekend until you have 6 to 8 solid Buyers on your list and at least 2 listings.

These are exactly the steps I would take to get my real estate business going. But I have an understanding that a lot of people don't think about. I think about planting seeds while doing the existing business. That seed planting will germinate and sprout tomorrow, or months from today. If I do a lot of seed planting while doing my other activities, I am storing up future business for later.

Here are some examples of planting seeds:

- ☐ Attract buyers, 2 per listing, to which 1 of those buyers I will need to sell something.
- ☐ Do an Open House: a lot of neighbors are thinking of selling sooner or later. Find a way to meet the neighbors.
- ☐ Meeting Strategic Alliances: If I keep top of mind, then these people will refer business to me. I keep top of mind if I refer business to them for certain.
- ☐ When I meet a FSBO, offer to do work for FREE and I maintain my professionalism. When their plan doesn't work, there is a good chance that I am the next choice.

- ☐ If I approach an Expired listing with a plan, with knowledge of their market and present answers as to why the listing didn't sell, they may not list with me right away, but I am on their mind.

I am constantly planting seeds. If you hang around me, you will hear me say something that I think is appropriate to the 4X Agent business philosophy that fits with the seed-planting ideal: "You can't control how fast a seed will germinate and grow—you can't pull on a blade of grass and make it grow faster, that is out of your control —but, you CAN control the planting. Focus on the planting."

While doing business to get paid quickly, always be thinking of the business that can happen down the road. Keep thinking of possibilities. Keep thinking in terms of serving. Keep thinking in terms of arming yourself with information, understanding, strategies, and product knowledge to becoming an authority so that you can give value to the people with whom you come into contact, and you will be amazed at how quickly that will pay off. Don't operate in a state of frenzy with no focus. Do not allow the state of your market, the conditions of the world, pandemics, market crashes, elections, interest rates, or anything that is outside of your control affect your activities and your focus. Always focus on the things that you can control. Watching the news to "be informed" can hurt you sometimes. Guard your mind and protect it, as if your life depends on it ... because it does. Your future depends on it. No person can be stopped who invests in his/her own mind. It is impossible to stop a focused person from achieving his/her objective. So, I encourage you to be that person. Be encouraged by that. You deserve it.

THE ART OF THE CONVERSATION

What do you think we get paid to do? What is the *one* skill that pays us the most? If you had to break it down to the basic core of what we have to do every single day — what would that be?

We talk. We talk a lot. We speak to a lot of people. The more people that we converse with, the better our chance of making more money — would you agree?

Conversing with people is what we do. So, as a result, meeting people is what we must do. As we meet more and more people, opportunities present themselves. Creating ways to meet people is your goal all of the time. When you are in a setting where there is a chance to meet new people that may need you, your mind has to be tuned-in to listen for opportunities. Remember, we are in the people business. Learning *The Art of Conversation* is a key skill to take advantage of, at every opportunity. I suggest that you set a goal to meet at least two people every day.

Our goal is to meet, converse and then convert. That is ultimately our goal — all the time. Every day, in all situations. Here is the process as I see it: It all begins with the conversation. A CONVERSATION with a person who may CONVERT into a LEAD or REFERRAL, which then turns into a CONTACT and then turns into a CONTRACT.

CONVERSATION -> CONVERT -> LEAD OR REFERRAL -> CONTACT -> CONTRACT

This is why the Art of the Conversation is the key in real estate.

We can meet people in many different ways. At open houses, we have an opportunity to meet both sellers and buyers. When we receive a phone call from our signage, we are meeting someone for the first time. The response you craft to an email inquiry on a listing, is the beginning of a conversation. Organized events are settings where people are in a mode of meeting and learning about each other; for example, the Chamber of Commerce or service organizations you may join, such as Rotary or Lions Club. It is important to be good at effectively conversing with people. In those circumstances, I find that a lot of sales professionals internally compare this to "speed dating." You are not sure how long they are going to stand there and listen to you, so you have to take that opportunity to tell them all about yourself. First, to get them to like you and then, wow them with how amazing you are, hoping they will stick around or become more curious to learn more about you. This is what most salespeople do. They are always selling. I was the same. I used to say this all the time, "We are not salespeople, but if we are selling anything, we are selling ourselves." I had to correct that mentality.

The truth is most people are truly more interested in themselves than they are in other people. They are interested in what they want to know. They are interested in talking about their favorite subject, which is themselves, their needs and the things that they care about. The funny thing is, we actually have that same urge. This is where you need to think outwardly and begin to win their trust and start the foundation of a relationship. The most memorable conversation to them, is one where they had a chance to talk about their goals and dreams and wishes and passions! When you give them the space to do that, you will solidify and create a positive experience with that person. You then become associated with that positive experience. Most people won't remember everything that was said in a conversation, but they will remember how they felt during that conversation. They will actually forget most of the words that you say. They will remember the important details, but all of the other stuff will fade. What *does* stick, though, is how they *felt* during that conversation.

The next challenge is knowing what to say. I find that this is always a challenge. Let's face it, we don't always relate to every person, or the synergy may not naturally be there, every time. If we aren't careful, we will fall into the habit of talking about something that is exciting to ourselves, but maybe not too exciting to someone else, just because it's easier. This happens when that person asks you a question about yourself that propels you into a four-minute tangent. The only time that is okay, is if they are like you and have the same interests. If they like all the same things that you like, then you will make a connection. But you can't rely on that, and it's too limiting to think that the only people you can have a good conversation with are people that are just like you. That will not help you grow your business.

Here is the first thing to understand. In an interaction where two people are having a discussion, it is important to be aware that the person who is asking the questions is the person in control. They're driving the conversation. You need to be the driver — not the passenger. So, how do you gain control? You ask the questions. When they give an answer or talk about something, let that spur another question.

Create a new habit. A habit of being curious about people. Become truly curious. Become fascinated. Become interested. Create this desire to know more about the people that you come into contact with. If you get into this mindset in every interaction and genuinely become a person who is curious about people, you will naturally ask the right questions that spur a conversation.

This is not easy for all people. This is not always natural, so it might take some practice. You can practice and learn. It is a skill that can be developed. The best thing about this is that nobody really knows that you are practicing. You don't need a "script partner." Every single person is your partner. Find an opportunity to do this every single day, and more than once.

Here are some ideas to help you get started and get you thinking:

- ☐ When you arrive at the office, say "Hi!" to the front desk person. Ask two questions about them and see where the conversation takes you.
- ☐ When you talk to your children about their day at school, see if you can ask questions to get more complete answers out of them...rather than "fine," "good" or "it was ok." Be curious. Ask and learn about their interactions with friends and teachers and get a deeper understanding of their lives at school.
- ☐ Talk with your spouse and ask more questions than normal. Go deeper. Understand his or her day a bit more. Share in the victories and defeats of the day.
- ☐ When you are in a restaurant, ask the server some questions about themselves to spur a bit of a conversation. Not in a creepy way, but out of genuine interest.
- ☐ When you go to the bank and interact with the teller, try to take notice of something to spur a conversation and try to leave that interaction, making an impression of some sort.

These are just a few examples but there are many, many, more. Start to see the world as a place of opportunity and see each person as an opportunity to chat. Just get into a chit-chat about something. The subject matter is less important than simply creating a habit of being chatty with people. Don't try to sell them a house. Don't try to sell them on yourself. Don't attempt to tell them all about yourself. Just practice having a meaningful human connection.

You may have heard the saying, "Practice Makes Perfect." But I say, "Practice creates new habits that will make your life better and pave the way to becoming more effective." I don't believe in perfection. There was only one person who walked this earth who was perfect. Here's another quote: "An ounce of practice is generally worth more than a ton of theory."

What types of questions are the best to ask? The quick answer is — whatever is important to them. Whatever will help you gain a better understanding of that person. First off, let's talk about the type of interaction. Let's face it, there are many ways that we come into contact with people. Every single time that we do, there may be an opportunity on which to capitalize. Nothing should be squandered. Based on your targets, you may have set a goal that you need to meet two people per day. Then make that the goal all the time — adding two people to your list every day.

Lists

How can we add people to our list? What counts? Who is "list worthy?" Everyone. We already know the 10-and-2 rule. So, if we know we are already eliminating 8 out of those 10, then we need to focus on the 10 in order to get 2. This is the 'numbers game' that everyone talks about. But I have also heard things like, "... for every 100 doors that you knock on, you may get two maybes." This is daunting and, I agree, the thought of that totally sucks. The reason for this, is that it is a cold and difficult "C" activity. The odds are stacked against you in those scenarios.

Contact Card

The first step was the list. Next is the Contact Card and then the working file. As you start doing things for people, you need a place to keep all of that work, research, and communication. These are active hot files. Some files may go cold and you may pick them up again in the future, so everything should be in there to remind you what you did for them before and the conversations you had. We will talk more about that later, but I want you to see the process. The Evolution. An **interaction** of some sort — to a **Name on a list**, to a **Contact Card,** to a **File,** to a **Working file,** to an **Agreement,** to a **Sale** and ultimately...the **Commission Cheque.**

If you have finished "Mindset Mastery" you know that there are so many different ways that you can meet people and leave some sort of impression. We can't possibly cover every single way to meet people, but I want to get across to you that there is always opportunity. In every setting, there is a chance to plant a seed. We can never control the overall result, but we can control the planting of the seeds. There are situations in your life right now where people would be considered, *Personal and Familiar* — these are people who are in your circle, in your dot. People who are within your "Sphere of Influence" and maybe a slight layer outside of that. People who are not part of your everyday lives, but who you see once in a while. You know each other's names, but it's a pretty surface familiarity. These are people who are perfect for practicing your conversing. Consciously think of ways to spur a conversation with them. Be genuinely interested and curious about them and get a deeper understanding of THEM. Do it and see what happens. Social settings, business meet-up settings, service organizations, church, volunteer groups, or sports teams of some sort; all fall into the category of "Personal and Familiar." These all represent opportunities. If they think of you as a high-quality individual, someone who is genuine and thinks outside of themselves, they will refer business to you when an opportunity arises. But you need to BE that person. Become that person. We attract to us what we are — not want we want or desire — until we become worthy of what we want or desire.

Resources and Referrals

There will be moments, when you have a discussion with someone, when you learn about what they do, and inadvertently meet other professionals who are in the business of helping other people in other industries, such as accountants, lawyers, financial planners, and other service providers. We deal with a vast array of clientele in our businesses and we run into people who would be perfect candidates for these people. We can be a fantastic resource for them. With that in mind, does it make sense to get to know their business philosophies, their absolute favorite and ideal clients, and get a clear understanding of what they can accomplish for people? Do you think that this could be of help to some people that you come into contact with? Listen and learn so you can capitalize on potential opportunities to connect people. If you become a connector you will become a valuable resource.

Now, you are positioned differently in the eyes of these people. You never know where a conversation will lead, but almost every time there is some sort of opportunity there, if you are listening for it. You may not be selling them a house today or listing their house today — but one day you will. Before that opportunity arises, are there other opportunities? Do they know someone who may need your assistance? Do you know someone who can help them with something? Do you know someone who would be an ideal client for this person? Do you know more about these people now, in order to become a person of value to them? This is how you create relevance. I would even go as far as asking the question like, "Hey, John...I run across people every day who may be a good fit for your business. Tell me, who is your ideal client?" Then shut up, listen, and make notes. If your philosophies align and you think this person will do good business and make *you* look good if you refer business to them, then actively try to steer people their way and see what happens.

Here is my take on referrals. I have seen people try to get money from other professionals, and vice versa, for referrals. This is crossing lines, in my opinion. From REALTOR® to REALTOR® is totally fine. That is how we make money. We disclose it to our buyers and sellers and it's all good. But once you cross industries, it gets a little fuzzy. Here is my approach on this. First, do you disclose to your clients that you are getting a "kick back" a "gift" or some sort of compensation, for referring them to this professional? If not, that is wrong. Here's the test. Think about if your client found out later. Do you think that they would be happy about that? If you are getting some sort of compensation and you actually tell your client up front, how do you think that sounds to them? If it were me, I would start to doubt that the person being referred to me, is best for me. It may cause your client to ask themselves: What is the motivation for the referral? Is it to get money from me, or is it to do what is best for me? I have had numerous service providers, such as financial planners or mortgage brokers, offer me a referral fee or some sort of compensation. I tell them that I don't believe in that. I just want them to do a fantastic job for my clients and do whatever it takes to "wow" them. Make me look good and that is all I need. I want my clients to feel that they can come to me, and trust that I will lead them in the right direction — always. I want them to feel that my motivation is to consistently create a positive outcome for them. This has always been the approach that I take.

Think of it this way...these people become your Strategic Alliances. Cultivate 10 Strategic Alliances and you will always have business coming in. If you got one referral a month from your 10 sources and added 10 deals a year to your business, that would that be a good thing! I have some strategic alliances that refer close to 10 a year to me — from ONE Strategic alliance! But you need to cultivate a great relationship — they must like and trust you and you must refer business to them. This is the law of Reciprocity. A 4X Agent understands the Law of Reciprocity.

If you are thinking outwardly, with real curiosity, and a genuine interest in other people, the conversation should be relatively easy. Remember the Mindsets that you need to employ. With more information you will be more able to figure out how to help people. Helping people becomes your super-power. In circumstances where it seems a little tougher to get things going, I default to something called, FORM.

F.O.R.M. – Family, Occupation, Recreation, Message

I learned about this around 25 years ago and found it to be extremely helpful. FORM has always helped me warm things up. Family...Occupation...Recreation...Message. Think of all the questions that revolve around the subject of FAMILY. Family includes loved ones, partners, other important people that may impact a buying decision or "life change" decision. The word 'Family' is simply to spur your mind into action. If you are talking to someone and they are alone, it may be a good idea to find out if there is another decision maker, as well. Or find out if they have children and what ages they are. This factors into buying decisions and life change decisions, for sure. If they are a single professional or they are relatively young — maybe parents get involved to help them. If they are newly single, is it from a divorce or separation or an untimely death of a loved one? These are all factors that drive a conversation in so many different ways. You can see how the word, family, brings with it so many different paths in a conversation.

That leads us into OCCUPATION. "Oh, so do you and your wife both work? Do you have to commute to your job? Has she looked into a transfer to this area?" Or maybe, we learn that moving to this area will allow one of the spouses to stop working. Is there a motivation there? Are they moving up or downsizing? Have all the kids left the house now and it is time to cash in on the big house and get into a gated community because they are retiring in one year? Motivation — help them set things up to retire well. Okay, we are starting to understand their needs and motivations a bit now. We can work with this. Begin to formulate a plan in your brain that can help them and hopefully this spurs more questions.

Next, we move into RECREATION. Recreation covers so many things. If they are downsizing, is travelling a burning desire for them? If they want to travel more, then maybe they want to live in a safe area where people are looking out for each other and there is low maintenance, where perhaps the landscaping is taken care of. If their children are big into football or hockey, then the type of school they attend may be a huge factor in the decision, which then affects the neighborhood that you have to drill down to. Understanding motivation is important. Are they really into golf or fishing? Maybe a hobby is the connection that you were waiting for in the conversation. This is where you could talk about yourself for a second to show that you relate or understand, as it creates connection. Relevance. They start to see you as a human being who is just like them. If you got to this point, you have earned the right to go deeper. They are letting you in. You will notice that their body language is much more different than it was at the start of your conversation. They are more relaxed and trusting.

Think of your interaction as a bunch of mini-goals and create mini-successes with each. My goal is to get into a conversation with someone, make a connection of some sort and just focus on enjoying the conversation. Then, they begin to start asking me questions about myself. They are so enthralled with our exchange, that they now genuinely want to know more about me. I have now moved past "sleezy salesman" to "nice person" to "someone they want to kno more about." I believe that I have now earned the right to take it to the next level. My goal now is to impress upon them that I am now someone who can be valuable in their lives. If I can get to this point, this is a "Contact Card" person. I now need their contact info to send *relevant* information to them, in order to help them. It should feel natural. In most cases, they feel the same way. This should always be your goal. Figure out how to serve.

M is for Message. Now, you want to get a MESSAGE across to them and it must be something that they want to hear, based on all the information that you just obtained. You may still ask some questions at this point, but these questions should be more about obtaining permission. Message

- *"Would you find it helpful if I sent you some information?"*
- *"Are you in the research stage right now? I find that people that are in this stage, need information in order to sit at home and do the numbers. So, I am happy to provide or I can put together some information that..."*
- *"It seems to me that .... is really important to you — let me get some more information on that for you." ---"Would you find it valuable if I did that for you?"*
- *"Do you need someone to help you out right now that knows this area well?"*

Use these check-ins and nod your head. Check-ins are like confirming permission. Nine times out of ten, they will nod as well and say yes. If you have effectively summarized their needs, then they will certainly agree. Why wouldn't they? It is all about them. You are a benefit to them. You have just spent the whole conversation trying to uncover what they need, their motivations, their why and what would be important to them. If you can focus on what you can do to help them in some way, you will see an amazing transformation occur. Levels of trust are being built, which creates the foundation for a relationship.

You don't have to be really special or have a "winning personality." It doesn't matter if you are a bit of an introvert or extrovert, or whether you consider yourself "shy" and "timid" because it's not about you. You are not a factor here. No matter how shy you are, if you are genuinely interested in learning about people and figuring out how to help them, then you will overcome your shyness. Any personality type can converse. We all need human connection. Making people like you also feels good. How do you do that? Learn to enjoy interacting and learning about others when the opportunities present themselves. They need you and you can be a valuable asset in their lives. Think of it that way.

Summarize what you have learned from them in your own words and ask them if you are on track. I literally ask, "So, am I on track?" I then begin to offer up my team to help them. I want them to feel that they are talking to the right person to get them to their goals, needs, and desires. I want to create a belief that I am the person to take away the stress, minimize the confusion and point them in the right direction and enlist the team of people to get them what they want or away from what they don't want, in some circumstances. If you focus in this way, you don't need tricky scripts and you don't need to memorize anything. We have established that People are People. Employing the Six Critical Mindsets and the principals of Mindset Mastery is all you need to do. Use FORM to help you get there.

MESSAGE

Now, if you get to this stage, there has to be some sort of conclusion, message or action you need to weave into the conversation. You begin writing down their information in order to help them. "Okay, super, so what's the best email for you? Can I get your phone number?...Did I spell you name correctly? What's your husband's name again?" Then summarize all of the things that you are going to do for them and tell them when you will get it to them. Then do it and let them know when you've done it, as promised. Send them a friendly text or call or video or all of the above, solidifying that you had a great conversation and check to see if there is anything else that you can provide for them.

MINI GOALS

Now, let's talk about the Mini-Goals along the way. Mini-goals are much like a football game. The Linebacker has a goal in every play. It may be a little different in each play, given where he sees the Quarterback lining-up or where the receivers are located. Are they in motion? He's watching all of these things and looking for clues. The Offensive Line and Defensive Lines each have a goal. They are also looking for cues. If the O'Line steps back with hands up, then it will be a pass. If the O'Line gets low and begins pushing forward, then it's a run. The receiver is either blocking for the run or running to get to an open spot to be available for catching a pass. His goal is to fool the defending corner. Make him think it's a run, so he takes a step forward, or make the corner defender think it will be a long pass, to get him over pursuing at full speed and then the receiver can stop quick and be open for the pass. The Quarterback is looking for all of these cues from the defense to see his opportunities. And this is all in one play! There is a combination of many mini-goals in one play, all happening in a split second. The ultimate goal in that play is to move the ball forward 10 yards. Then they get a new set of downs and it all starts again. But the ultimate goal is to score a touchdown. Very rarely does a team score a touchdown on the first play of a drive. They understand that. If every team tried that every single time, then it would be easy to defend, wouldn't it? They understand that it's all about mini-successes. When mistakes are made, then corrective actions or adjustments have to be made. It is not about just that one play ultimately. After the Fourth Quarter is over, it's the mini-successes throughout the whole game that created a team's victory or defeat.

I'd like you to think of your business in the same way. It's all made up of mini-successes and mini-goals. Focus on the little mini-goals and you will learn, improve and then apply. Learn and apply and you can't go wrong. Sometimes, things won't work out like you were hoping and sometimes, you will make mistakes. That's okay. Take corrective action and make some adjustments. I found that when I broke my real estate work down into mini-goals, it was easier to analyze where I messed-up. If I look at it as a whole, I have a harder time getting to the points where I need to make some adjustments or take corrective action, because I am looking at it as one large event.

Imagine this — a football team loses the game, and the coach is getting interviewed with the reporter asking him why he thinks that they lost. "Tough game today," says the announcer. "Why do you think that you lost the game today, Coach Bryan?" The coach answers, "Well, I think the reason we lost was because our defense let them score more touchdowns than we were hoping. So, that sucked. Also, our offense scored less points than the other team. So as a result, we lost. Go Raiders!" That would be ridiculous, wouldn't it?

Remember, we were talking about all of the different things that are going on in one single play. There are a lot more reasons why a team loses. In each quarter, small crucial events were happening. There are times when the defense changes their coverage at the wrong time, and the offense capitalizes on this. Or somebody who's really good gets injured and then a rookie who doesn't know the position as well has to step-in. There are many, many reasons. So, it is important for the team to get together on the Monday morning and sit and watch film. They will peruse every single play and analyze the little nuances of each; and the players will learn from this. They will learn how to watch for certain cues. They will learn and apply. They will learn corrective action. They will work on the skillsets during the week and then they will study their next competition and work on continuous improvement.

This is what we all need to do. Get out there on the playing field and take action. Get into as many conversations as you can for practice and then think about those interactions later. Replay it in your mind, so you can learn, improve and tweak.

Just like in football, we want to achieve a bunch of mini-goals, and we have to celebrate the mini-successes. Have you ever seen the "Special Teams" guys who only get on the field for kicks and punts? They are fired-up. When they tackle the runner before he can get to the 25-yard line, they are jacked! They run around bumping into each other, celebrating like crazy and bouncing around. Did they win the game? No. They just achieved a mini goal within the game. Think in terms of that.

Here are some mini-goals that I would work on using an Open House, as an example: Meet a person, make eye contact and decide if this person is worth engaging.

1. Engage in conversation...First goal...they think that you are a nice person.

If they leave at this point, then you have achieved the goal. They think that you are a nice human being. Celebrate!

2. You get to go deeper. You learn more about them. You are actively talking about them and have a nice conversation. You have learned about them. You found common ground and began to relate somewhat.

If they walk out at this point, then you have achieved a goal where they will remember you. You went from *nice human being* to *someone who is memorable*. You never know what will happen. You may see them again. Hopefully, they have filled out an Open House form, so it would be alright to contact them, re-visit the conversation and see if there is something that you can do for them. Celebrate!

3. You get into a deeper discussion. You know about their family dynamics, how their working environment affects their lives. You may have made a good connection. They aren't doing anything for some time. They were simply curious. But you have permission to keep in touch.

This is a great seed that will germinate later. Make sure you fertilize it. You are memorable for sure. This is the beginning of a *relationship*. What are the opportunities here? Set them up with your team and a mortgage professional. Send them info. Get them into your world now. If you do things right in this stage — there is a chance that they will refer someone to you before they even do a deal! Wouldn't that be awesome? Success!

4. You have graduated from *Guy or Gal at the Open House/ Door Opener/ That Listing Agent* to *Nice Human/ Interesting Human/ Memorable Person /A Professional who can really help me out.* A *Valuable Human*.

Just like a football game. The Quarterback starting on the 20-yard line close to his own end zone, rarely will try to go for a touchdown on the first play. He knows he has to work his way down to the opponent's end zone, and the team knows, as well. They have four downs to get 10 yards. So that's the first goal — make 10 yards or more. But even if they only make 2 yards, they have another "down" or chance to get the remaining 8 yards. You see, there is no failure or bad outcome.

In conclusion, I encourage you to think about real estate in this way. Hopefully, you will have more than one person attending your open house. If you have four groups or four people come into your open house, then that is your four downs, and you only need one. If you got one out of every open house that would amount to four to eight each month. You can't help but make $100,000, if you achieve that on a monthly basis!

The Art of the Conversation is all about earning your way to the next level. Rather than practicing scripts, practice conversing with people. Practice getting to the "heart of the matter." Practice asking lots of questions and create a habit of infectious curiosity. Create a love for people. Learn how to appreciate all personality types and put pressure on yourself to learn what you need, in order to figure out how to help them. Let's face it, you are not going to sell them a house today. Resign yourself to that. You will sell more houses when you figure out how to serve people where they need to be served. Solve their problems and challenges. Become a person of value and then you will inadvertently become a person of success!

GET LISTINGS

I have found that when someone is either starting out or struggling in real estate, the biggest challenge is having a good inventory of listings in order to make money and generate more business. We all understand that business begets business. Once you have business, it is easier to get more business. You need something to leverage.

Part 1 — The 3 "L's"

LEADS. LISTINGS. And LEVERAGE. Generating LEADS is a skillset that needs to be mastered. Learning this skillset will be interwoven throughout all of our lessons and, as we get deeper into the course, you will begin to discover new confidence in your ability to create, generate, integrate, and facilitate leads. Getting leads will become less of a worry and your attention will then be more focused on servicing and facilitating the leads. This is where we want to get to.

For now, we need to help you get your first two LISTINGS so you can figure out how to LEVERAGE those listings in order to keep the ball rolling in your business. Getting into momentum is what you want. It's like a car with a standard transmission. First gear gets the car moving but when it gets to a certain speed the RPMs increase and the car is working really hard, so you have to change gears. Then, when you get into 5th gear, the car is barely working but it has a lot of momentum. So, in the beginning there will be a little bit more frustration and "revving up" but just keep in mind that it will get easier. The amount of hard work in the beginning *will* pay off. You will realize the benefits of The Three Ls in time. Always keep that in the back of your mind.

Now let's go back to the lessons in the "Quick Commission Blueprint." Remember the four activities that you need to do before embarking on a mission? When the US Navy Seals were going after Osama Bin Laden, they had to prepare properly. They had already been well-trained. They knew their target. They spent a lot of time diligently gathering intelligence and creating an understanding of the environment they would be entering into and did months of surveillance before making a plan and executing it.

What is your mission? Did you do your homework from the Quick Commission Blueprint?

- ☐ Did you fill out the form?
- ☐ Did you determine your target?
- ☐ Where do you want to focus?
- ☐ Did you complete the worksheet?
- ☐ Do you know the price point that produces 40% of the sales in your market area?
- ☐ What is the most dominant product type to focus on?
- ☐ If we can find sellers in this target area given those aspects above, what do you think those people (sellers) are most likely to buy?
- ☐ What is the price point and product type for that type of seller?

Most of the time, the seller needs to know where they are moving to before they sell their existing home. If they feel confident that they will be able to find their next home, they will be motivated to sell. Would it be good to study up on that part of the market as well? Yes — this is how you become a specialist. Now as you progress in your journey as a real estate professional, you will begin to learn about other areas and other market types but, for now, drill down to where you should focus in the interest of efficiency. Remember, the other reason to hyper-focus on where most of the business is occurring is to take advantage of another phenomenon: "Frequency Illusion."

Remember our talk about "Frequency Illusion?" The more you get, the more you see; the more you see, the more you notice: You become literally tuned-in. So, it makes a lot of sense to take the time to figure out where to focus. Flesh it out and get a clear understanding of the market.

Not many people really focus this way. They only focus on the end result. But there are many paths to get to that result. Just simply focusing on commission cheques isn't enough. Why do you think that is?

Well, if you focus on the commission cheques, then everything that comes into your view will seem like an opportunity to get one. You will take any listing and do open houses in the middle of nowhere for the senior agents. You will hop in your car and drive to meet a buyer at the drop of a hat, with no pre-qualification. You will become a "door opener," because you are focused on commission cheques instead of drilling down to the specific business that will *actually* be the shortest distance to that commission cheque. Believe it or not, those activities could potentially take you away from the result, because you are chasing something that isn't tangible. When I explain "Frequency Illusion," I ask the listener to think about a type of car. Not just any car. We see cars everywhere, all the time. But, if you buy a green Volkswagen Jetta, you will not only notice more Volkswagen Jettas but you may come to think that you bought the only green one and, yet suddenly it's like all of the green Volkswagen Jettas migrated to your city and appeared in front of you! It is the strangest phenomenon. This is what I mean. Focusing on what you want has to become a habit.

I don't want you to believe that you will suddenly, magically, manifest all of your business out of your head. It won't be as easy as focusing really hard and then—poof! — success appears in front of you. That is not what I mean. But I do know that your mind needs to clearly understand not just "focus," but actual "hyper-focus" that keeps you connected to the correct opportunities. The opportunities are already out there — you just have to tune into those people, strategic alliances, comments, moments, exchanges, and interactions that help you access them.

Let's take this plan and literally walk through it.

Remember our scenario? Let me remind you: I got into an airplane and literally jumped out into thin air and landed in a community that I have never been to before.

Pretend for a moment you open up the Google Earth program on your computer. What do you see? The whole earth. Then you type in North America. Google moves you to the North American continent. Then you type in *United State of America*. And then you type in *Oregon*, for instance. Then, let's say I am floating down in my parachute to a place called Salem, Oregon. I land in a place called Morningside Park.

Now, I have actually done this on Google Earth. It is important for you to know that I have never been to Salem, Oregon in my life. Okay, so I am floating through the air and I notice some government buildings, a penitentiary, a few churches, some schools and university buildings. I am now in Morningside Park and looking for a real estate office to start my career in Salem, Oregon. I get on my cell phone and do a little research on the town. I quickly learn that the average income is $47,000. I check out a website that tells me that most jobs are in the health and education sectors and in governmental employment. That information tells me that these are mostly middle-class families living here.

I don't have access to the licensee real estate information yet, but here is a quick paragraph from REALTOR.com, as of the date of my adventure:

Homes for Sale in Salem, have a median listing price of $329,900 and a price per square foot of $185. There are 1,481 active homes for sale in Salem, Oregon, which spend an average of 74 days on the market. Some of the hottest neighborhoods near Salem, OR are West Salem, South Gateway, Morningside, Four Corners, Northeast Neighbors.

I have now quickly determined, after being in this community for about 15 minutes with fairly limited research, that my target market is double-income families earning a combined average income of $90,000 to $120,000 per year. These people want to be near parks and schools. The greatest is currently people in their mid 30's. Most of them are either nine to five Monday to Friday people or shift workers. I checked out the Morningside area and it is a low crime area with all of the amenities that people in this demographic would like. The price point of the product in this area ranges from $270,000 to $420,000. This is a great price point for these types of families. Most of the product-type is single family homes ranging in size from 1400 to 2500 square feet in nice, safe neighborhoods. This is the product I want to market. I will meet more buyers and attract more opportunities with this product-type. So how do I get listings?

First, I would start with expired listings. I know that listings take an average of 74 days on the market to sell. A lot of listing agents only take 90-day listing contracts, so if they were slightly over-listed for 45 to 60 days and didn't react quickly enough to the market, they might not have had success. They would most likely also experienced a higher level of frustration with their agent. This is where you can come in and be the hero! Let's say there are 10 "Expired" in the system right now. Do you have a way to obtain those numbers and learn whether or not they are on the "Do Not Call List? If so, I would take these steps:

- ☐ Research market activity.
- ☐ Study the old listings and read the comments to see if there are some aspects of the home that could be improved upon.
- ☐ Pull off all of the listings that SOLD, that were comparable to my clients' home and study the data on those homes.
- ☐ Look at what is active right now and go and view those homes.

I know this seems like a lot of work, but what you are doing is making yourself relevant. You are arming yourself with knowledge and understanding and this will serve you when you get into conversations. You are becoming an expert in this market. Not yesterday, not tomorrow, but today! Remember, I have literally just landed in Salem, Oregon after jumping out of an airplane, so I am compelled to get knowledge like this as soon as possible. Acquiring information should always be first priority for you. Eventually, this habit will become second nature. Now you are ready.

#1 – Check at the office and see if there are any listings in the neighbourhood you want to work.

Ask the listing agent if you can do open houses in this neighbourhood in two weeks. If there are none in this neighbourhood, do an open house somewhere else. But if there are opportunities in your neighborhood of choice (or landing zone in my case), then get that booked.

#2 Do up a letter.

We have some examples in the Tools area for you. Put the letter in an envelope and handwrite on the outside of the envelope, *Mr. and Mrs. [their name],* if you can get that information. I would hand-deliver this letter and, if they aren't home when you get there, leave the letter in the door with a card inside.

#2a – If they are home, chat with them a little bit. This could be an opportunity to offer them more pertinent information on market activity for homes like theirs (while they were listed) and what the current competition is. You may have that information with you, but you can get their email address by promising to get that information to them. GOAL: Find a need in the conversation. See if there is some sort of motivation there and get a meeting booked for another time to talk about how you market homes.

#2b – If they aren't home and are not on the "Do Not Call List," then follow up the next day with a phone call.

See the script at www.4Xformula.com/attractbook to help you. GOAL: Convince them that you are different. See if you can uncover some sort of motivation and book a meeting to chat, go over market stats, and let them know how you would market their home to get them the best possible result.

#3 – Phone call, see script at www.4Xformula.com/attractbook.

#4 – Hand-deliver flyers in the neighbourhood.

This flyer will let them know about the upcoming open house and will also invite them to come one hour early to get a sneak preview before the public arrives. Have some snacks and refreshments for them. Make sure you hit all the Expired and FSBOs in the area, even if they are a distance away. Make sure you get flyers to them. These Expired Listing leads need to be contacted a minimum of five more times. However, if they tell you they will never list with you or they are not selling for a long time and have decided not to sell, you can stop and put them on the back-burner program, but not until they tell you that.

A good real estate agent finds a way to bring value to a client. When we cover working the neighbourhood, I will unleash plenty of ideas for you to engage the community; but, for now, let's take things step by step. My main goal is to get you into a groove of activity; we'll fill in the details as we progress deeper into the material, and eventually you will have a definite workable system. One example is to create weekly activities for Expiries and keep abreast of them on a daily basis. You may come to the conclusion that the Expired product is not in the right price target or attracting the right target buyer or seller may not be worth the extra effort if it takes you away from your target area.

Now that you are on top of your target Expiry efforts, go back two years and look for Expiries that occurred over two years ago and did not go back on the market. Most likely, these homes were on the market for a reason at the time that made sense. If the owners didn't put the home back onto the market and decided to stay, there may be a story there. It's worth contacting these people and having a chat to see what you can uncover. Maybe there is a way to help them now, if their situation has changed and they are now ready to sell. Because they've already been listed, there is data in the system. You may be surprised to learn that there is some low-hanging fruit there! Let them know that you are now the neighborhood real estate professional and you want to learn as much as you can about them so you can figure out how to help them if they need it. You want people to be able to rely on you for honest information that will help them make a concrete and workable plan.

Part 2 - For Sale by Owners. FSBO

These properties are a great resource for getting listings. FSBO's! Yes, the infamous FSBO: The person who thinks that you have no value at all. You charge too much, and they can save that money and do it themselves because, hey! Anyone can sell real estate, right? They are convinced that they are effectively cutting out the middleman and putting more money in their jeans.

This is a tough one. It starts out as an “us against them” mentality so it may take a slightly different approach to convince them to work with you. This is very delicate operation, but if you can get good at this and convert 20% of the people you approach, you can really do well! This is the goal.

What do I mean by that? Every 2 out of 10 people. Eight of them will not work with you or anyone for that matter. Just accept that. It’s also very possible that they have a real estate agent to whom they are somewhat loyal, and they are simply trying to be FSBOs for a while to see if they can “save some money.” When it’s time to list, the urgency grows, and then they have an agent they’ll call. That is okay. Praise the fact that they are loyal and tell them something like this: “*if someone does a good job, provides excellent service, gives quality advice, pays attention to details and really, truthfully works for the clients’ best interest, well, then of course client loyalty would be a by-product of that by default.*”

See what you just did there?

You just set the qualifications that THEIR Agent should adhere to! Without actually *saying* it, you are telling this person what a real estate professional IS, and how they should operate. Which how YOU operate. He may think to himself, “Wow...I don’t think *[my last real estate agent]* really operated that way fully. I mean, I like the guy...but he didn’t really do anything last time we sold our place, and he made a boat load of money.” You never know how they will internalize those thoughts, but it’s okay. You have planted a good seed and have also inadvertently let them know the level of service that you would provide, in spite of not expecting any kind of loyalty. See the message there?

Okay. Back to the strategy. Remember that the FSBOs are sellers. They are in *our* world now. They are selling their home. Paradoxically, just about every single FSBO seller will allow you to sell their home. FSBOs have a common interest: they want a buyer to buy their home. Normally, their contact information is easy to find. You can find it either on a sign in the front yard, on a few FSBO websites or on Craigslist, Kijiji or Facebook. But if they are looking for buyers, they need to make it easy for a buyer to contact them. They are giving permission for someone to contact them. Do you agree? So, contact them. Why not?

Now, let's take a moment to discuss the mindset I want you to have when you contact these people. First, I accept that they may be getting a lot of calls from other agents. Secondly, I accept the fact, that they are understandably suspicious that we may try to talk them into something. Thirdly, FSBOs are either afraid of a debate or ready for a debate. Fourthly, they are fully convinced that anyone who lists with a real estate agent is an idiot.

Here is what I know: I do this for a living. This is my business and I am a professional. The fact is, I can make their lives easier and help them get what they want. They simply don't know what they don't know.

But today is not the time to try to convince them of that. We have a mission, which is to list two homes as fast as possible and plant seeds for future listings at the same time. This is our Modus Operandi. Always. Constantly.

Every contact point has three potential outcomes: NOW, NEVER or LATER. That's how I think of everything. NOW, NEVER or LATER. If there are 10 FSBOs you have chosen to tackle in your market area, there has got to be at least two NOWs and most likely six NEVERs and potentially two LATERs. That's how I think about. Does that help you?

During the initial parts of this strategy, you are actually qualifying the home and the seller *before* making a decision to list this home. If you have the feeling that you are not even 100% positive if you even WANT to list this home until it meets your criteria, then that creates a different posture.

Do you agree? Think of it this way: if you have a criterium whether or not to list a home, it eliminates the desperation of needing the sale and puts you in the driver's seat. You are now simply doing research to create your own conclusion. And the conclusion may be that you do not want to list this home. 60% of the time you won't list the home. You are looking for the two NOWs and planting seeds for the two LATERs...

Okay...so now we go into preparation mode. We determine the listings that are For Sale by Owner, in the market area and bearing the price point we believe is most attractive to buyers. Having already been listed, these homes have data available in the MLS system. History, price, title search, tax assessment—all can be found in the MLS. It costs a little bit of money to pull a title search but it's worth it. For example, I can find mortgage information, evidence of previous litigation, multiple liens on the title, or if there is more than one mortgage on the property. More times than you can imagine, I have pulled a title search and learned that these people were on the verge of foreclosure, were in the middle of a divorce or were leveraging the home by using it as an ATM. Sometimes the exact opposite picture is revealed. The owners are in a great position: There is no mortgage on the title and they have lived there for 10 years, during which and the equity has tripled. All of this information helps you get a bit of an understanding about the story behind the house. This is information you don't want to bring up right away. Just keep this to yourself for now.

Local tax authorities write up to assessments to create a value for properties, for the purposes of the determining the annual property taxes payable. I am not sure how it works in your state or province, but the assessments are normally based on fairly limited data. You shouldn't have difficulty obtaining this information. Tax assessments can help you in your research stage. The seller receives notice on a yearly basis of the basic value of their property, which may have increased or decreased depending on the marketplace of the previous twelve months. A tax assessment is not an official appraisal but, for some reason, the sellers tend to think of it as valid proof of value for their property. The truth is, this assumption is not really very consistent in most cases, but it does help an agent get an understanding of what the seller may be thinking in terms of pricing.

Next, I usually do a limited Comparative Market Analysis (CMA) and have this information ready for when I contact this FSBO. I am not sure how far the conversation will go so I want to be armed with the information in case we get deeper into the process. Keep in mind, there are some scripts and scenarios you can download to help you with the conversation: www.4Xformula.com/attractbook. My goal on the phone is to treat the FSBO like another listing agent in my marketplace. They are in the business of selling a house; I am in the business of selling houses. This is my marketplace. I specialize in a product. I work with the buyers who may want to buy this product. I am the neighbourhood specialist in this area and it is my business to know about all the product price-points in this marketplace.

It's as simple as that. I have personally viewed every house on the market that fits these criteria. I have researched the whole neighbourhood. I know the type of people that live here, have created Avatars in my mind of the people who will want to move here. I have thought about the product they are selling in order to move into this neighborhood and I have thought about the product that the people selling in this neighborhood will potentially want to buy if they leave this area. I have made it my business to research all of this. So, it makes a lot of sense that I simply want to view any FSBO home as just another home for sale in the neighbourhood that I specialize in. I make it my business to know everything about this neighbourhood. Do you get my drift?

Do you understand what I'm saying to you about approaching an FSBO? Does this give you more confidence, thinking about it this way? Does this simplify the process for you? Keep it simple. Your goal is to simply make an appointment to view the home. Five minutes. The FSBOs are showing the home to people all the time. Let them sell you on the home. You are not sure if they qualify, they could be totally nuts, totally out of whack in terms of pricing. OR, as I have run across many times, they are actually too low! This is a fantastic opportunity for you. You don't know until you see the house and meet the person. You may choose to take it to the next step, if they qualify. Is this a home that you would like to put your time, money and effort into selling? AND, are they the type of people that you would like to work with? This is a very simple approach. You are qualifying *them* to see if this is going to work for YOUR business plan, for your mission. Remember, all you want is two FSBOs, the best two. Is this going to be one of the two? That's the question you need to be asking yourself.

Always keep in mind, we want to break things down into mini-successes, little stepping-stones. There are stages to relationship. Let's not get confrontational at the beginning. Let's not start peppering them with questions right away. Doing so puts people on the defensive. We want to minimize the defenses. Use the Trojan Horse strategy: Get in the gates first before you release your army of questions and tricky scripting. Book the appointment. Don't even call it "an appointment." Call it a visit. Here are some ways to ease into this visit:

- *"Is there a time that works for you, for me to visit your home really quick?"*
- *"Just let me take a quick look at it so I can have it my mind, in case I run into to someone who may be interested… "*

- *"Can we schedule a time in the next day or two, where I can come by to get a quick look, so that I determine if your home could potentially work for one of my Buyers? I just need about 15 minutes or so...so which day works best for you..."*

  This kind of conversational approach takes the threat away but also lets the FSBO know that you are serious about what you do.

You are a professional. A real estate professional who deems information to be really important. You are willing to make the extra effort in order to serve people well. You are different. They have most likely already spoken to real estate professionals from other companies; agents who are trained with tricky scripts have already tried to convince them to use an "expert" to sell their home. There are many good reasons to offer your services. Do you agree? I do, too. I am totally convinced that they need me. Are you? Good.

But, the thing is, now is not the time to get into it. Not yet. Right now, I want them to think that I am a little different. I'm not desperate. I'm someone who is confident and knowledgeable, someone trustworthy. Someone who is simply interested in bringing a Buyer for their home. That is the desired outcome for them.

Okay, so that's the first goal. Get a chance to check out their house. How do you prepare for that five-minute meeting? Well, you should have already done a little bit of research so that you understand where the house fits in the market, in terms of pricing and marketability. Now you need to see the home to confirm a few things.

When you show up, be on time. Be dressed nicely, but not overly dressed. Don't be threatening. Help them to feel comfortable. This is human connection time. You are now entering into their world. This home is where they are comfortable. Nurture this feeling. Surprise them by not asking them anything about the marketing of the home, even if doing so goes against all the sales training courses out there.

Remember the stages of relationship. Remember the Mindset Mastery Bonus section. Remember *The Art of Conversation.* The five-minute meeting with the FSBO is where you begin to apply those principals. Are you with me? What did you tell them the purpose of the visit was for? To quickly view the home, right? What do you think they are expecting you to do? What do you think? This is really important. If you want to be different then I would suggest that you don't do what they expect you to do. Don't do what everyone else does.

You are there to view the home. Ask questions. Learn about the home. Ask them what they love about it. Ask them about the neighbourhood. If you notice some updates, ask them for details, and then praise them for their good taste. Focus on the home. Be enthusiastic about it. Really make a huge effort to find things to compliment them about. This will break down the barriers.

You can talk about price expectations. You can check in to see how you would be compensated if you brought in a buyer. Fundamentally, there are only two ways you'll be paid: out of the sale price at which they are offering the home OR as an addition tacked on top of the sale price. It is good to see where they stand, as far as compensation is concerned. But just keep it to that. You want to come across as a person who is an equal to them. They are in the business of selling a home and you are in the business of selling homes, that's it. Treat them as equals. Be high energy, engaging and friendly. Don't let awkwardness take hold of the energy in the room. Overcome it with positive energy. As you give them compliments and praise and maintain consistency to your stated purpose, you will begin to see the barriers coming down. It will happen.

I would suggest one more thing. Keep F.O.R.M. in the back of your mind. Family, Occupation, Recreation, Message. See if there are opportunities to open up a conversation with them. They may decide that they like you and begin to ask you questions; if that happens, then its game on. Go into F.O.R.M. Gather info. Learn about them. Uncover motivation and then get to the message part where you can do something for them. Get their email and promise to do something for them that is valuable to them. But don't force it. This is not your only chance to speak to them. You will create another opportunity to get into a deeper conversation if you leave with your mission accomplished. View the home. Meet the owner. Leave an impression that you are different. That's it.

If you leave at this point, you have accomplished the goal.

OK? Can you do this? Yes...anyone can do this. It takes no special talent or salesmanship to accomplish this task. This is totally achievable.

Part 3 — Research and Action.

Have you found value so far? Have I asked you to do anything that is uncomfortable or "salesy" to this point? Do you feel empowered to go and meet people now? Can you implement these plans into your real estate business immediately? You can.

Let's go back to Part 1 just for a second. Let's re-visit the parachuting adventure for a moment.

I jump out of a plane and land in a basic subdivision in "small town USA." It's a fairly normal town, Salem, in Oregon. The challenge is to land there and start my real estate business. I have no pre-conceptions, no contacts, no family, no friends, no history, nothing. I am a complete stranger. In fact, if we are being perfectly honest, I actually have kind of a weird back story: "Ya...um, well, I got in a plane and decided to jump out of it and then I decided that wherever I land is where I will do business. So. What do *you* do for a living?"

This would be a very strange way to introduce myself. But don't forget that the parachute story exists to create a scenario in which I have no advantages at all. Nothing. Zero is my starting point.

That's the true test, isn't it? This is what real estate agents want to know: "How do I start? What are my first action steps? Just tell me and then I will go and do it." Do you agree? Did we achieve that? After absorbing Parts 1 and 2, do you feel confident that you know the action steps to apply in order to get business happening? Do you think that you can schedule activities in your calendar on a weekly basis to move the ball down the field?

Imagine, I am now two weeks in this new community and doing my first open house event, employing all of the tactics and strategies. I would argue that I know as much about this little community's listings, sales and social activity than a lot of the real estate professionals who have been operating in that community for years. Especially in the "Morningside" area of Salem, Oregon. That's because I have made it my business as a REALTOR®-PRENEUR to learn all I can about my target marketplace.

I want to encourage you to adopt this new mentality. Treat your market area as if you just landed there in a parachute. You have enough money to last you two months and that's it. You are hungry for knowledge and want to learn as much as you can about the people who live here. Erase all of your pre-conceived notions about your marketplace and commit to re-learning and understanding your market. This way you create a new curiosity. You become more sensitive to things and your hyper-focus becomes activated. You streamline your efforts and start to attract business. There is absolutely no doubt in my mind.

Now, with that confident mindset, let's get back to real life. Take that certainty we just spoke about and now apply it to you and your market area. Can you do that?

The truth is, you do have a past. You have a family, friends, a history. You have outside interests that have put you in front of other people. You have an understanding of the area, its schools, parks and its activity centers. You know about local shopping and traffic patterns and how the different seasons roll out. You have attended local events such as 4th of July celebrations and been to concerts and Christmas parades. You have attended school concerts and been involved with sports teams. You have bought a car or bought a suit; you shop for groceries and you go out for dinner or coffee in this area. Perhaps you have served as a volunteer in some way or have a church that you attend. You have a bunch of buddies over to watch the game on Sunday afternoons. You have enjoyed neighbourhood barbecues or "cookouts." You have a life here. Maybe your spouse works somewhere in this community and has met a few people that are now in his or her life, as well. There are already a lot of people who you touch base with every day who can lead you to an opportunity. Are these people who would do business with you or refer business to you? Do they know how serious you are about real estate? Do they know how committed you are to being successful in this business? Do they like you and trust you?

We will get into database management later but, for now, I want you to think about your contacts. In truth you have a "percolating dot." You do. There are real estate deals to be gleamed from this. Think of all your contacts as bonus business that is available to you now or will be in the future. If you are not already utilizing a database management program, I would open up an excel spreadsheet and enter as many people as you can into that. Names first, email second, phone, and other contact info in the columns after that. Make your contact list a live document that you add to constantly. Make it a new habit. Jog your memory. You will be unbelievably surprised at how many people you actually know.

If we calculate the actual people that we "know", what do you think that number is? It has been studied that after we are about five years old, we begin to recognize people. So, from this early point in life, you can safely say that we "know" people. The average person knows between 300 and 600 people. Does that figure surprise you? Some people know many, many more.

Let me ask you this: out of 300 people, do you think that there may be one or two who need to sell or buy a home in the next 30 to 90 days? I have personally scrubbed my database on an annual basis and still have over 400 people in my database. These are people who have done business with me and I believe would do business with me again, forget about all the people that I know. Sometimes I see someone and have no idea which part of my life I know them from, but I recognize them. It happens to me all the time. This drives me crazy. Or even worse, someone says my name to me (...this actually happened the other day...): "Kelly Johnston! How are ya? Good to see you!"

I had no idea who this person was, but he knew me well. He obviously saw the confused and stupid look on my face, so he said..."you don't recognize me, do you?"

I sheepishly answered, "Uh, no... I got to be honest...I don't" He told me his name and, as soon as he did, it all came back to me. I hadn't seen this man for almost 30 years! He had changed drastically. His body type was totally different and he had long hair and a short beard. Nothing like his "look" 30 years ago.

This happens to me a lot. It is so embarrassing. But here's the thing: I have signs all over the place. I was in the newspaper with listings and even had an ad in the local movie theatre years ago. I have been in real estate since 1997! I am out there.

People are going to remember you more than you think as soon as you begin to get yourself out there in the community.

They kind of have an unfair advantage, don't they? But that's a good lesson. That man who recognized me was working in a retail store. What if I treated him or his co-worker like crap? It turns out we were actually having a nice discussion and joking around a little bit. That's another reason it is important to conduct oneself appropriately, utilizing the right mindsets; because you never know. You never know who is listening or even just watching.

If you are new in the business, starting to build a database management program should be the first thing that you do. Most offices will talk to their new agents about this. If you have started on your own database, great. Here is a link to this book's accompanying website: www.4Xformula.com/attractbook. Download the tool called "Mind Triggers." Think of all the people you know....now, surely there is someone who needs your help. This is a great start. I am not saying that this is the only way to build your business. Not at all. In fact, 90% or more of your business is going to come from what I refer to as "unmet friends." But, at this stage in your business, databasing is really important.

In the 4X Formula Quick Commission Accelerator, in the GOAL SETTING module I talk about the amazing Olympic Athlete Usain Bolt. In that module I explain the importance of *starting well* and then *finishing strong*. Good database management is what makes that trajectory possible. Imagine six months down the road, you run into someone who should be on your list, someone who you could easily have found an excuse to contact in some way. Do you know what I mean? I mean, something as trivial as a quick text or a phone call or a pop by or something, okay? This is a person you know but you don't see all the time. But you bump into them at the grocery store and you have a great conversation and, in that conversation, he innocently announces to you that he and his wife just bought their first house.

Oh, man. Feel that for a second. Let it sink in. Let's take it a step further for a second. You inquire about their real estate professional, and they tell you it was this lady named *Martha Buyer's Agent* and she was nice. So, you say to them, "Oh that's great! How did you meet her?" and one of them answers, "Oh, we met her at an open house." AAAAGH! It wasn't even a friend or a family member!! Feel that. Let's move the knife around a bit, let's pour some salt in there: "Aaaaagh!" The pain. Feel that.

How much is your average commission on a deal in your area? $3500? $5500? $10,000? That is what it cost you for not getting your name out there.

Do the work. Utilize the "Mind Triggers" Tool and get this done. Approach all of these people and let them know you are open for business. Get this done. Make a decision to contact every one of these people in some small, non-threatening way. Gently let them know you are in the business of helping people buy and sell homes and you'd like to help them out one day, when the time is right. Do this. In the beginning, I would reach out to people five times *per day* as a minimum. Do this. Do it. Don't leave things to chance. Stack the cards in your favor. Give yourself the best odds of winning.

Alright, we have gone over a lot of information and check listed activities that need to be done, so let's recap and summarize all of this this into actionable steps. Let's break this down into bite-sized chunks.

The first stage is the Research Stage. Drill down to the product type you want to focus on. There is some work and focus involved here but there is so much information available to you, much more than when I began my career in real estate. It is amazing how much information you can obtain in 10 to 15 minutes now, online. It's all there! Isn't that exciting? These tools are here for you...use them.

#1: Price Point: We look at the most popular price point. Where are 40% of the sales occurring? Sheer volume of sales.

#2: Product Type. What type of real estate is selling the most in that price range? It may be two different product types. Pick one, at first, and then begin to specialize.

#3: Buyer Profile. Get an understanding of who the buyer is. Create an Avatar in your mind. Go to your city's website and see what you can learn. There is a lot of information there. Find out demographic information, average income, average age ranges. Where are most of the jobs are in your area? What areas are less subject to crime and, therefore, more desirable for your target market of buyers. Get clear on who your buyers are so you can begin to speak their language. What other services would be attractive to these people?

#4: The Seller Profile. Begin to understand where the sellers are going to want to move. Why are most of them selling? This may not be your biggest concern at this point but pay attention. Make it your business to learn about how to help these people. Figure out what gets them excited for their next move. This will be the next product-type in which you'll want to specialize. It's all about the "game plan." Remember, some people don't want to sell until they know they'll be able to buy what they want.

#5: Get out and view all the homes that fit with this trend. See every one of them. Make notes, check sales to get an idea of market trends.

What skill sets do you need to work on to start enjoying success in these efforts? Nothing special. To quote Marshawn Lynch, from the Seattle Seahawks, "It's all about that action, boss." It's all about having the correct focus.

After the Research Phase, here are the Action Steps:

#1: Book an open house two weeks in advance. Put a marketing plan together. We will get more specific about this plan in "The Master of the Open House" chapter later on. For now, get out there and do it.

#2: Research Expired Listings and determine the ones that you want to go after. Put a plan together to simply meet the owners and view the home. That's it. Don't try to get the listing yet. Just meet at least one owner with an Expired Listing. That's the goal.

#3: Same thing for FSBOs. Get at least one meeting. Don't try to get the listing, just focus on getting one meeting with the owners. View the home and qualify it. Determine if this is the one that you want to list.

#4: Read through the scripts at www.4Xformula.com/attractbook that we gave you for this module. Read them over and over, at least 20 times. If you'd rather use a different script that suits your personality better, then re-type them out in "speak writing," using the rhythm that you speak. Then read that and over again. These scripts are designed to help get you started. Personalize them with your "mini-goals" in mind.

#5: Start your database excel spreadsheet and begin thinking about all of the people you know. Download the Mind Triggers to help you fill up that list.

Okay. There's a lot of work to do. Practice all 10 of these steps over the next few weeks and then move on to the next chapter. Don't be afraid to go out there and mess up a little bit. Don't be afraid to run into a few little challenges. At the same time, believe it or not, you will actually experience some successes to celebrate as well, which will keep you going. Focus on the little successes and when you have some setbacks or minor challenges, think about how to correct them for next time.

We will deal with some of these challenges and corrections as we move along in the program, but this is a "working course." Here, we roll up our sleeves and get to it. We have to stretch ourselves every day. It takes 21 days to formulate a new habit, so we have to get on this, every day. Also, it is absolutely critical now that we read over our goals three to five times per day. Read them slowly. Say them out loud. Read them quietly to yourself, using different levels of volume at different times of the day. Try different paces and rhythms as well. You have to mix it up or else it gets too monotonous.

You are a "Goal Getter," and you know "Why." I have absolutely no idea about your "Why" but it's not about me. It's about you. Your "why" is custom-made for you. You, INC. You are The REALTOR®-PRENEUR and this is your powerhouse. Schedule out the 10 activities and hammer them off. Get it done. Then do it again. Then do it again. This is what you do now.

Before we move on to more Skills and Strategies, the next Chapter is designed to give you a better understanding of our habitual behaviours. How to transform ourselves by changing some of our habits. Russel Wilson from the Seattle Seahawks – SuperBowl Quarterback – said in an interview early in his career, before he had won a Superbowl, this statement and it has always stuck with me:

"The Separation is in the Preparation."

Prepare yourself for success. In every aspect of your life. I love that simple quote because it is so powerful.

THE SEPARATION IS IN THE PREPARATION

"If you pick the right small behavior and sequence it right, then you won't have to motivate yourself to have it grow. It will just happen naturally, like a good seed planted in a good spot."
–B.J. Fogg

Preparation Habits

It's all about the power of good habits. I know that you are creating mini-successes already. You are feeling more and more confident. You have identified your market, studied the product type for your market area and are well armed with knowledge and understanding. You are becoming more and more relevant to the people that you come into contact with. You are getting into the habit of having conversations with people you run into on a daily basis. Learning more about people is becoming a new habit.

Keep doing this every day. Have at least one really good conversation with someone else where you learn about them. Don't limit this conversation your comfort zone. I'm not talking about your spouse or child or best buddy. I want to encourage you to have a conversation with someone you have never met, someone new. It's a crucial step in the process of 4Xing your real estate business.

Remember, you are in the habit of continually planting seeds. You never know what these seeds will manifest into: referral, a future business a strategic alliance. A listing. A buyer client. You have no idea. Forget about the result for now. The results will come; for now, just focus on the planting.

Have you ever heard of the Horsetail Weed? This weed can grow anywhere. It is extremely obnoxious. I happened to find one growing in my backyard in a golf course community. The one turned into a whole bunch of horsetail weeds all over my yard. Suddenly they were everywhere! I asked my neighbor, who is an avid gardener, what to do about it. She told me that the only solution was to "move away." The reason they are so hard to eradicate is that their roots go down as far as seven feet underground and then they all connect in a subterranean root system; then, the plant sprouts up above the surface in many different locations, without rhyme or reason. The Horsetail weed: That's an analogy for what *you* are doing, planting the seeds to create an "underground network" of business that will eventually pop up into the air.

Having a Horsetail Strategy creates bonus business that comes to you over time.

We are what our habits make us. You have created a new habit of reading your goals to yourself every day, at a minimum of two times per day and reading over your WHY worksheet material at least once per day. These activities start out as obligations, but if you work at them every day with intention, they become habits. It's like brushing your teeth every day. Have you ever left the house and forgot to brush your teeth? Have you ever done this? It feels horrible! Brushing our teeth is something that all of us do every day at least once and a lot of us, twice a day.

But back then in the early 1900s, this wasn't the case. Not everybody brushed their teeth every day. Dental practices were a lot harsher back then. I mean, they literally had their foot on your shoulder while yanking on your tooth to get it out of your mouth. It was a horrific experience to go to the dentist back then, yet, people were still not in the habit of brushing their teeth. You'd think that the horror stories about dental rot would have been enough of a motivator! It was a real problem.

The toothpaste companies of the day tried scare campaigns, publishing articles documenting the dental issues of the day. They actually spent millions and millions of dollars trying to get the general public to simply brush their teeth. The companies expected people to react to their campaigns and rush to the corner stores to get toothpaste and start brushing. Who wouldn't want to improve their teeth, if the solution was as easy as brushing, right? However, it wasn't until they put a little mint into the toothpaste that the companies were able to change people's habitual behaviour.

It was that fresh minty feeling afterwards that actually caused people to get into the habit of brushing. That fresh feeling in their mouth. The difference between morning breath "mung mouth" to the "fresh mouth" feeling, is all it took. When people brush their teeth in the morning now, it is less about ensuring that they maintain their teeth and more about the feeling afterwards. The fresh mouth feeling. The immediate feeling. The immediate result.

So, we know that in order to create a new habit, we need to have another benefit. We need to create a feeling that we enjoy, love, or even crave, in order to solidify that new habit.

Creating a new belief, is part of this. Once you have this new belief, it feels good. When you begin to visualize what it will be like to enjoy this new lifestyle, it feels good. When you start to see the possibilities, it feels good. When you begin to be empowered with strategies, it feels good. When you have a nice conversation with someone and leave that conversation with a smile on your face, that feels good. When you do the work and prepare, and then reap a benefit, it feels good. When you suddenly have someone ask you a question about the real estate market, and you have the answers because you have been studying it, that feels really good. When you get your first listing, or attract a buyer at an open house, that feels good. When you get that commission cheque and deposit it into the bank, it feels good. But what's actually happening neurologically is that your brain gets a little "dopamine hit" when these things happen. and associating the actions and the feelings solidifies those habits. And that leads to new beliefs.

These are all positive things. These are feelings that you want to feel over and over again. Eventually, you understand that it is *the repetition of positive habits* that creates these new dopamine rushes. Your new habits get you to those positive, endorphin-filled feelings, reinforcing the reason that we took on these habits in the first place.

"Successful people are simply those with successful habits."
-Brian Tracy.

That is why the WHY is so important, why the GOAL sheet is so important. We need to feel the way we will feel when we achieve those things, first. Think deeply about this. There is a good reason why I talk about this so much, why I keep dwelling on this.

Understanding the Brain

There are three parts to our brains. We have the conscious part, the subconscious part and our active nonconscious part. Our conscious brain is the input.

What we see, what we hear, what we think, and what we feel in the moment, is the input. Meanwhile, our active non-conscious brain is working in the background, according to our programming. Our self-talk, our inner thoughts, and the information from past influences and experiences all come from the conscious part of our brain. Our subconscious is the recorder, taking in and dispelling the information that goes into our brains.

Remember when I was talking about the past? I was trying to explain the reason we need to write out our WHY worksheets in the first person, using the language of the *now*. This is crucial because the recorder—the non-conscious or sub-conscious part of our brain—does not discriminate. It doesn't know yesterday, today or tomorrow. It doesn't choose or judge the information. It just records the information. Then the active/non-conscious brain takes over, creating the sense of reality that we store as "experience." I tell a story in the course about when I was 12 years old playing soccer. I was a Goal Scoring machine when I was young. But that year I moved up to the 12/13 boys league, and my coach told me that I should NOT expect to score as many goals. Just like that, the seed was planted in my brain. That year I hit goal posts, crossbars, and missed the net. I was still able to create the opportunities to score but that little belief in my brain held me back from actually scoring. That is how powerful our brains are. A similar thing happened to me again, later in life. This was about 17 or 18 years ago, when I was golfing at a particular golf course, called the Golden Eagle. This golf course has a long waterway that snakes its way around the course. I had a horrible slice in my swing, in those days. I have corrected it somewhat now, but it was really bad back then.

Well, I lost 18 balls that day. 18 balls! One ball per hole. It was unbelievable! But my slice was only part of the problem that day. My main issue was the water. It was dominating my mind. I couldn't focus on anything but the water. If the water was on the left, I would hook it. If the water was right in front of me, I would flub the shot. If the water was to my right, I would slice it. You see, I was controlling the input. I was focusing on the water, focusing on what I *didn't* want to happen. I didn't want the ball to go in the water but the more I hit it into the water, the more I hit it into the water.

I should have been focusing on what I wanted. The nice green smooth grass. Focus on the grass. Focus on the grass. My self-talk should have sounded more like this: "Whenever I hit the ball, it always goes on the grass"… "I enjoy hitting the ball best from the Fairway"… "The *grass* is my focus… that is all I want to focus on"… "This is where I hit the ball to… the grass over there."

We need to program our minds to be thinking about the things that we want. The life we want. The income we want. The things we can see, visualize, and attach emotion to become manifest. The reason your GOAL list is so powerful is because you created it. You. This is custom-made to you. You took the time to think about it, dream about it and write it down.

Now, if you take the time to write down your dreams in the first person and in the language of now, and then read them over and over again, something incredible will occur: the active non-conscious part of your brain—the part that gives you hyper sensitivity, and will, and attitude—will literally be infused into you, until suddenly the results begin to show. When you run into old patterns or have minor setbacks you will move things forward, make corrections, and improve. You'll start to notice details you might have overlooked before, and you'll find yourself benefiting from the Frequency Illusion.

Don't short-change yourself on these exercises. Learn to control your thoughts. A 4X Agent operates with intention; a 4X Agent is in control. Writing out your goals, and writing out the life you want on your WHY worksheet and reading it over and over again, is one very important way to learn how to operate with intention and gain control over the life you want. This is not a warm, fuzzy feel-good thing. This is intentional, and life-changing; has the power to help you in your life by programming and re-programming your mind. Then you will experience amazing success in your life.

We are in the ATTRACT section of our course. It is called that for a reason. We focus on the activities that cause you to attract what you want.

Here is one thing that I know for certain: There is this little voice in our heads that speaks to us, all the time, no matter what. Most of the time we don't notice this voice. But it is there. Pay attention to it. This voice is a product of our programming.

We are programmed. Don't believe me? Let's test it out. Say these words:

"I make $900,000 in gross commissions every year!"

What happened? If you have never earned $900,000 in commissions in a given year then your little voice of doubt will creep in and say, "No, you don't. You have never earned $900,000 in commissions."

That little voice is your current programming. That is okay. Just keep in mind that it is there. This is why we have to write our goals and dreams out on paper. We have to visualize and feel what it is like to achieve it. We have to read it aloud every day multiple times per day...until that little voice starts to go away and you begin to have the belief. That is the first part.

The other benefit that will begin to happen is, your active non-conscious brain will activate and begin talking to you. When you feel like slacking off, you will hear a new voice, a different voice. It will speak to you like this: "You earn $10,000 per month, you can't slack off." Or it might suggest, "Lock in two buyers for every listing; here is a person on the phone right now...try using F.O.R.M. and see if there is a way that they can be helped... Ask questions, be interested in this person and see what happens." Suddenly you become "hyper-focused" and you begin to see opportunities and step up your game.

I wanted to discuss this with you at this stage of the book because you have now embarked on the journey. You are getting active now.

In the last chapter, I gave you a lot of activities to do. I have been encouraging you along the way, gently prodding you. But the truth is, I have no way of knowing if you are actually doing the activities. I have no idea.

But here is what I do know. I know you are going to run into challenges. You are going to have doubts. I know you already have past-programming and, possibly, other habits that are maybe not serving you and your business. I know that little voice will be speaking to you. I know that it takes hard, intentional work to create new mindsets and new habits to replace those old ones. I know this with absolute certainty. So, at this stage, it is crucial that you believe and trust in the process.

I only want good things to happen for you. I want you to experience your best outcomes, to succeed and smash through your goals. I want to hear about your success stories.

But this is not about me. It is about YOU. *YOU, INC.* right? You are driving the bus. You decide where the bus is going. You decide who to ride on the bus with. You decide to put the pedal to the metal or put on the brakes. You decide where and when to fill up the gas tank with fuel to keep the bus going. Only you. Where you end up and how fast you get there is totally up to you.

Okay...do it right now. Look over your goals. Read over your WHY worksheet. Close your eyes and see it. Feel it. Experience it. Then read over the scripts and get to work with the steps that you have to complete today to move the ball down the field.

Get yourself ready for that opportunity. Make that phone call to the next person you are going to meet. Anticipate success. Expect success. Be ready for it.

The next chapter is the Pre-Listing Interview. See you soon. Go out and make it a great day!

THE PRE-LISTING INTERVIEW

PRE-LISTING PREP TALK

I know you have been out there putting into practice all of the principals we have been going over. Are you taking action? To succeed in anything, we have to PLAN to succeed. Right? Planning requires information. The Pre-Listing Prep Talk is no different. It will help both parties clarify the plan and work on solutions and action steps to achieve success.

Next, we need to be working skillsets....and always be in motion. Always in action. FOCUSSED ACTION is more productive. Focused action: a plan formed by the seeking out, gathering and interpreting of good information. Another one of the benefits of action is that we inadvertently learn, improve, apply as we go. Nothing happens until action is taken.

Okay--quick check in. Do you really know the market you are going after? Have you met with a FSBO? Have you contacted an Expired Listing homeowner? Have you created a new habit of conversing with people and learning about them? Are you reading over your goals every day? Is your

.el of belief growing? Are you feeling more and more confident in your ability to meet your goals? Have you started to create new habits and are upping your game? Are you working with intention every day? Have you met with a Mortgage Professional or two?

If you haven't completed any one of these steps, then go back and spend some time on it. This course is not a race, it is a journey. We need to experience all aspects of the journey together for maximum results. Okay?

Let's continue. First, let's revisit the characteristics of the 4X Agent again. A 4X Agent is someone who has integrated most or all of the above steps into their lives and businesses. Does that make sense? Test yourself: When you don't feel like doing something, or you wonder why I am teaching a certain element of the course and not sure how it applies, read over this list. So, when I say: "Hey, all you 4X'ers!" ask yourself: "Am I worthy of being called a 4X'er?" I know the answer to that. YES....is the answer. You can be. Anyone can be. It's a decision. That's all. You paid money for this book. I assume you want to apply the steps that I teach. I have every right to have that expectation.

Okay, let's go over the list together:

1. A 4X Agent is a professional
2. A 4X Agent is accountable
3. A 4X Agent is organized
4. A 4X Agent maximizes their time
5. A 4X Agent is intentional
6. A 4X Agent is consistent
7. A 4X Agent builds relationships
8. A 4X Agent receives referrals
9. A 4X Agent is in control.

If you are doing all of these actions, you can't help but experience success. You are already beginning to gain confidence. You are already 4X'ing your business. It's happening!

What about the 12 points of Power? This is OUR 4X Agent Manifesto! Here they are:

1. A 4X Agent understands the Law of Sowing and Reaping.
2. A 4X Agent is in full control of their business
3. A 4X Agent enjoys life while netting more money than they need to survive
4. A 4X Agent makes a plan and works the plan according to the goals they have set out
5. A 4X Agent is accountable to those they serve and to themselves equally
6. A 4X Agent works smart and hard at the same time because time is precious
7. A 4X Agent is consumed with Belief
8. A 4X Agent understands that action overcomes fear every time
9. A 4X Agent expects challenges and faces them head on
10. A 4X Agent understands the Law of Reciprocity
11. A 4X Agent intimately understands the Power of Multiplication
12. A 4X Agent has Mastered all four facets to build the dream business.: ATTRACT – ATTAIN – SERVE – RETAIN.

I love this quote from Charles Schulz – *"There is no heavier burden than an unfulfilled potential."* Let's fulfill your potential!

Once again, I want to re-enforce that becoming a 4X agent and adopting the 4X Agent Manifesto is something that anyone can do. The only obstacle to this manifesto is yourself, and your own limiting beliefs. Adopt these principals and you will be on a path of constant Improvement. The path to the BEST YOU. I can guarantee that. The money and success will follow.

Today we are going to talk about the process of preparing for appointments. When we get into ATTAIN, my second book, we will go over the actual meeting and how you WIN the business. I fully expect that you will already have had a few appointments with potential sellers before getting to the ATTAIN section, and that will have already enjoyed success or maybe struggled a little. And that is just fine. But don't hold your breath and wait for ATTAIN! I encourage you to get out there and just get at it. When we get to that section and go over strategies to win, it will mean a lot more to you, and you will see that these strategies work because you have been out in the field in motion taking action! Make sense? This is when training moves from simply theory to practice. No effort is ever wasted. No meeting is ever a waste of time.

I know that if you are employing the right mindsets and strategies we have gone over up to this point, you are already better off than most agents out there in the marketplace. Be proud of this. You deserve it. Good for you if you have already met with some people. Remember the little successes and celebrate them. Your conversion rates will get better and better as you progress. It took me many, many, years of making mistakes to get to the point where I could coalesce this information for you. I am going to save you time and a LOT of pain. But *you* are going to have to invest some time and experience a bit of pain in order to get better. There is no shortcut for the good work.

This Chapter is designed to help you deal with the common scenario's that we experience once we begin to ATTRACT people to us. Here is a typical situation: You have had a conversation with someone about listing their home. They have expressed interest in listing their home. There are many ways that this situation could play out but start here: You are a person who properly prepares for meetings. Right? This is the moment where you slow things down and your mission is simply to obtain as much information as you need to prepare for the meeting. We have a tool for this called the Pre-Listing Worksheet. (Go to 4XFormula.com/attractbook.) This form will work to help you with your scripting as well as help you remember the things that you want to know and keep you on track.

These clients may have been on your Lead Tracker form, rose up to a "contact card," and now you have followed up and set up a meeting to discuss what you can do for them. This is not the time to "sell them" on how great you are. This is the time to be different than all of the agents they have dealt with. Most agents just go to the appointment and talk about all the things that THEY want to talk about. They are prepared for THEIR agenda, if they are even prepared at all. But not a 4X Agent. We build rapport. We build trust. We are organized. We are in control. It's okay to allow the conversation to drift off a little bit if the other person wants to chat about unrelated topics, but you want to stay on track. Be a good listener but also stay focused on real estate. The clients will respect that you have a process and they will appreciate that you take them seriously. [We will discuss Value Proposition, marketing plans, and overcoming objections, such as the "commission talk" and "pricing the home" later on, in *Attain*. Those courses are loaded into the members area].

Hopefully, you will already know some of the answers to your clients' questions due to prior communications with these people but, just in case you get a cold call through the office or a neighbor calls you up out of the blue, you are going to need to get the get the conversation back on track. One way is to repeat some of the information you've already gleaned from earlier meetings back to the clients:

"So Linda, I think I remember from our last discussion, that your plan was to move to Denver, is that still correct?"

However, it is possible that you get a call from someone who you have not been able to interact with yet. Suddenly, a call comes in. This person has their own expectation of how the conversation is going to go. They may be thinking that they are simply calling to book a time and then get off the phone. They may think that THEY are going to ask all the questions and "pre-qualify" you before making the appointment:

"Yeah, this is Chuck over on Blank Street and I got your note when I got home.... hey, so.... what's the commission? What do you think my home is worth?" Chuck thinks those are the most important criteria for listing a home, price and commission. This is common. He is thinking that he is going to do all of his business on the phone. We don't do business on the phone. We don't make decisions until we have the proper information. We need to know whether or not we even want to work with this person. Would you agree that there is not enough information to get into any kind of discussion about those things? But how do you address those questions respectfully and tactfully, thinking on your feet?

Here is what you might say: *"Well, I will tell you, that the commission part of it is up to you. But we will get into that when we get together and I have to be honest, I have no idea what your house is worth until I see it personally. It wouldn't be fair to you if I just threw out a number. To be honest with you, I think that would be disrespectful."*

The commission is up to him. The essence of the transaction is the details of how the buyer's agent will be compensated. But we'll get to that later.

You go on: *"But, Chuck, I will tell you that if you are calling because I left a note, then I have identified your home as something that I think that fits with the target market that I am currently working with right now."* This is totally true, isn't it?

"You know what, Chuck, I am excited to sit down with you and talk about what I do, and how I differ from other agents, but I would like to take a quick moment to ask you a few questions so that I can properly prepare for when we do get together. That way we can have a great meeting and you will have everything you need to make a great decision. Does that make sense? Does that sound fair?"

And get right into it. Start asking questions. Use FORM. **You can work off the Pre-Listing Prep worksheet,** It keeps us in our lane to get the information that is important to help us prepare for the meeting. Their answers to these questions help us drive the meeting when we meet with them. Remember, the WOW factor for them is that you show yourself as the agent who meets their criteria.

Remember to use FORM. Remember to be conscious of their personality type. Remember to listen for clues of past experiences so that you begin to understand their frame of reference. Preparing for the listing meeting and winning the listing is in the next sections of our course in ATTAIN. But first, we have to go over more strategies you can use in discussions like the above.

Your Goal is to meet this person, at their home. In order to give them accurate information to rely upon for their plan, it only makes sense. If you can convince them of that and get an appointment booked, you have succeeded. That is something to celebrate! The Pre-Listing Prep worksheet will help you prepare for that meeting. It will help you ask the right questions, to gain valuable insights. Now the logical next step is to see the home.

It is easy to discuss the Commission, when you are able to discuss in full confidence what you do to help them achieve the best result. We cover this later, but it is important to get out there and get into those real conversations first, and you will begin to gain clarity on what is important to these people. Start thinking about formulating your value proposition. Start researching what all of the top agents do to sell homes. What tools do they use? What service providers--photographers, Video, 3D or Drone companies--are in the area? How can you get professional brochures made?

Remember our scenario? I just dropped into this little town called Salem, Oregon and I started my real estate career. I identified my market and started to contact FSBO's and Expired's. I held an open house. I received a call from someone who wanted to talk about listing their home.

This is how you create momentum. This is how I imagine my first month as a licensed Real Estate professional who just dropped into Salem Oregon. I picked up a buyer last weekend, in fact, at an open house and I am now working with them. Now I am looking for service providers in the area to help serve my clients well. I have spoken to two mortgage professionals. I am starting to formulate my value proposition and my marketing plan for my first listing meeting. I have spoken to two owners of FSBO homes and have had at least two conversations with Expired Listings. I have viewed every single listing in my category and I go out and view homes every day. I am now putting into motion my next Open House event. This is exactly what you will be doing, as a 4X Agent, using the Attract model. Are you with me!? I hope so!

In the next chapter, we are going to tackle the open house. Then we'll segue into the following chapter, "The Neighbourhood Specialist." This is the farm where you will be planting the most seeds when you are starting out. All your efforts are designed to work in concert with this purpose. The OPEN HOUSES, the EXPIRED, and FSBO's in this neighborhood will get to know you. This will be the core of your business, your bread and butter, over time and you will continue to nurture this area and everyone will get to know you and trust you. We will cap off *Attract* by talking about the Neighborhood Specialist because that's where you'll be working your magic. We're going to go over more intentional material and I am going to help you make a Five-Year Plan for your Farm so that you will experience a bumper crop of leads from your area. Excited? I am so excited for you. Go out there and make a great day!

MASTER OF THE OPEN HOUSE

Hopefully, you have already performed at least one open house. Maybe you haven't had an opportunity to book one yet. Maybe you've been doing open houses for years... you might even have one booked for this weekend!

Part 1 – Intro to the Open House

No matter where you are on the open house spectrum, we are going to begin at, well, the beginning. Okay? We are going to cover every aspect of the open house process so you can discover how effective it can be.

I remember when I was really busy in 2005. In those days, I had a partner. He used to love to say to our listing clients, *"Open houses are a waste of time. Open houses don't sell houses."* Sheesh. That used to really embarrass me. But I think this is a fairly common mentality: that open houses are something that new real estate agents do if they don't have any business. Maybe they think sitting in an open house for two to four hours is a waste of time. Both of these attitudes have merit, I suppose, if you think that all you need to do is show up, put a sign on the front lawn and hope some people materialize.

But that's not for me. I don't like operating on *hope*. Remember, successful 4X Agents like to stack the cards in their favor. We maximize our time because time is precious.

Let's look at some of the reasons agents don't like doing open houses. Is it because they are boring? Do they feel open houses are a waste of time? Are they avoiding open houses because they have better things to do on a Saturday or Sunday? I actually heard one popular real estate trainer on YouTube say, "some of you don't want to waste your time doing open houses because you would rather be out "prospecting."

What? Knocking on 100 doors to say, "Hey, are you interested in selling or buying in the next 30 to 90 days?" is a more productive activity than doing an open house? This is a cold business. You are bothering people with nothing to offer them. You are, basically, being a door-to-door salesman. You are the reason that people have "No SOLICITING" signs on their doors. It's true.

Let's look at the reasons that these same agents WILL do an open house: Because they are obligated to? Because they committed to doing it for their seller when they listed the home? Because the house hasn't sold in 60 days and the seller is getting desperate? Because their seller demanded it?

Do you love doing something because you have to? Do you get a lot of joy out of doing things out of a feeling of guilt, or to placate someone's stress? Personally, I don't. I have done it and I do it. But I don't like it. And I'll bet you—Successful Real Estate Agent—don't like it, either.

I am going to assume that you are a lean, mean 4X Agent machine who wants to succeed and increase his or her dollar per hour, over time. We are different from the rest. We know that open houses can be a wonderful tool for generating business. Open houses are not a prison sentence or a community service obligation. The key difference is you—as a 4X Agent—are working with a plan. Remember? You are working with a plan that we set in motion at the beginning of this journey and you understand that the open house is crucial to the process that you are working on now. The open house is simply the next step in the execution of the plan.

Let's look at a 4X agent's ultimate open house objectives:

1. To meet prospective buyers.
2. To meet prospective sellers in the neighbourhood. This is a seed-planting activity, but you have to be conscious of opportunities in everything you do. You can plant a seed for multiple future listings in a single open house.
3. To market the home to a prospective buyer and meet other buyers to sell houses to. You never know who might show up...or what you can learn from a conversation. They will either buy this house or another house that you help them find later.
4. To market the home to prospective buyers who may be working with other agents. If you get a chance to meet a potential buyer with an agent, you can negotiate well for your seller. You can encourage agents to send their clients and you will protect their commissions. If a buyer represented by another agent is attending your open house, then it's your job to represent your seller to the best of your ability. It is game on! Get them excited about the home, and humanize your seller, so that when their agent prepares the offer, you have set up appropriate expectations with that buyer to help the negotiation position for your seller.

Think about this: You are a nice person. If you create a picture in the buyer's mind that the sellers are very nice people, it's going to be more difficult, later on, for that buyer to be as tough in the negotiations. Humanize the process. Create a little edge.

I'd like to address some other advantages that can come from staging an open house. Let's call this the Secondary 4X Objective: Building your reputation. There are four main pluses that can come from an open house:

1. People are getting to know, like and trust you.
2. You are impressing new people with your confidence, the depth of your research, your marketing and your decisiveness.
3. You are meeting the people to this neighbourhood and are gaining a better understanding of their personas and their profiles.
4. You meet at least one Buyer not working with another Agent who needs your help.

Here are some statistics from the National Association of REALTORS® (NAR). I found this very, very interesting. Here is what we know: 89% of the homes that were sold and 89% of the buyers who bought homes in the U.S.A utilized the services of a real estate professional: Nine out of ten people. 75% of them, in both categories, worked with the first person they came into contact with. Put simply, three out of every four buyers or sellers decided to work with the first real estate professional that they met with.

Does that tell you something? Is that exciting to you? On the other hand, there is a one in four chance that, even if someone has met another agent already, you can be second choice. Remember that. They may mess up. That agent may tick that person off at some point. I have benefited from this, many times. I literally had this scenario happen to me not long ago. I had a developer call me up directly. I had just happened to be on a series of long calls that day. He called but didn't leave a message, which always makes me wonder. Was it a sales call from some company trying to sell me something? Anyway...he tried me four times, so I thought that I would call him back. He didn't answer but I could tell he was a regular person from his message, and I left him a voice mail. I apologized for having been busy on the phone and told him that I would love to help answer any of his questions but, since he hadn't left a message, I was unaware of the reason for his call (See? I am training him for the future. Let's be efficient and leave information so that I can prepare and call you back with what you want next time).

Anyway, he called me back about 30 minutes later and we ended up being able to chat. As it turned out, he asked his agent to request information on a small development property that we had listed for sale. The truth is, we did get a message from the agent two weeks prior and I told her where to get the info. We always make it very easy for agents to get information on our listings. I texted the agent and told her what to do and asked her if she wanted to chat about the property. I also left her a voice mail message. I then checked back two days later to see if she got the info and if she wanted to discuss the property. I never received a return call or even a text from her confirming receipt.

Long story short, she failed to get the information from the simple source that we have available in our system. Then she had the audacity to tell her client that *we* neglected to get the information to her. Oh, boy. I needed to straighten things out on that front right away; so, I explained the chain of communication to him. This developer has now asked me to work for him in finding development properties. Our listing didn't work for his purposes, but he was impressed with how we responded and how we conducted ourselves. It was all about that one in four chance I mentioned two paragraphs back. I did not bad-mouth the agent who ghosted me. I told him the truth. We sent him the info within 15 minutes of speaking and discussed the details of the development. These were all details that I was willing to talk to the other agent about, but she never took the time to call me back. Instead, she left the door open for her client to seek out the information another way. They had a history, she had sold him three or four properties in the past and most likely had a sense of entitlement with this client. Well, I am afraid she will now be learning a very costly lesson. There is no such thing as client entitlement. She breached trust. She dissolved the relationship.

Now, let's be honest...nobody is perfect. This happens to all of us. The stats tell us so. But just understand that as long as you are accessible, engaged and willing to do what you say are going to do, you can create opportunity for yourself. Okay...let's move on.

Here is another thing that is incredibly interesting...60% of buyers and 70% of sellers in this survey said that the most important criteria for choosing the agent, was Number 1, **Reputation**. And in second place was **Knowledge of the Neighbourhood.**

Now, let's go back and summarize. From the Quick Commission Blueprint chapter to where we are right now...what have we been working on? We have been focusing on the top 40% of sales in our community, right? We want to work in the neighborhoods, view all of the homes, and meet the sellers and buyers who make up 40% of the sales in our market area. This is our focus. What have we also been doing? We have been focusing on making ourselves absolute specialists in this category. We have been making it our business to know about every single listing in this price point. We have viewed every single home. We have met people in the neighbourhood. We have located all of the FSBO's and EXPIRED's in the area we are focusing on. You have been increasing your Knowledge of the Neighborhood. Is it important? Well, apparently it is very important to the people that you serve, as it should be.

If you have completed the action Items, then congratulations on your work so far! And remember our four secondary objectives; these are all about building your reputation.

Remember the parachuting scenario? I have been focusing on my "landing zone", in the Morningside Park area of

Salem, Oregon. I have made it my business to learn everything that I can about this area: the basic demographics, the homes on the market, the buyers who want to move there, the people who are selling their homes there. I know all the stats and I have viewed all the homes. So, let me ask you this: Have I satisfied the second criteria for both buyers and sellers?" Have I displayed knowledge of the neighbourhood? Yes...in my first month, I believe I have. In my first month! But I have only been here for 30 days. I haven't really had a lot of time to build up my reputation yet. That's next. But think about that stat: 75% of buyers and sellers who utilized the services of a real estate professional started working with the first person that they met.

Now, let's talk about what "meeting someone" means. Bumping into someone accidentally is not meeting someone. Dropping a flyer off at a door doesn't count. At your open house, just telling people to look around and then waving goodbye when they leave does not count, either. Remember the *art of the conversation*. Remember F.O.R.M. You need to get deep enough into a good conversation with someone to find a need, or a challenge, or to simply gain understanding of their goals. That is "meeting someone." Getting contact information and eventually arranging a time to discuss helping them? —*that* is a meeting.

By the way...this is what we get paid to do. Practicing *The Art of Conversation* is constantly on our minds. And the stats tell us that three out of every four times we do this, we get paid for it. Right? So...If you get a chance to meet someone, you have a 75% chance of winning their business, even if you haven't had time to build your reputation yet! Does that get you excited? It does for me. That means, all you need to do is create an opportunity, even if that only means being in the right place at the right time; if someone is thinking about selling or buying, then you have a 75% chance of being the one who gets to take care of them. Then, you will do an amazing job. You will operate according to the 4X

Agent standards and with the 4X Agent Manifesto in mind, and will build relationships and enjoy abundant referrals from clients. Your reputation will grow, and it will get easier and easier as time goes by because you are building, and planting, and growing...constantly. Right? Are you with me?

Let's take that N.A.R. stat, 75%. Three out of four buyers and sellers. Now, this statistic applies to all two million agents in the United States. This is taking into account all types of business. Do you think that all of these people are in the top 40% of sales? I don't think so. Consider this, because it is really cool: We are only focusing on the top 40% of the MLS sales. The most active part of your market. That means we have actually multiplied our odds because we are only zeroing in on the highest sales and the most interested buyers. So, do you think that we have increased our odds of meeting and converting more leads into buyers and sellers than the average real estate agent? Yes! Your odds are better than the stats. I have absolutely no idea how to do the math on this, but I know that the odds are better.

Here's why I know. Let's use this metaphor: I am playing one-man poker. I have a deck. The dealer has a deck. We are playing against each other (I know this would never happen but, for the sake of the metaphor, just indulge me on this.) Let's just say I was allowed to add an extra Ace, King and Queen into my deck. I have a better chance when the cards are dealt, right? Now, what if I removed the lower numbers? You know, the twos and threes and fours and fives...what if I just took them right out and replaced them with more Queens, Kings and Aces? Also, I get to bet on my hand before the flip. The dealer I am up against is playing with a regular deck. Who has a better chance of winning?

That's the point of this lesson. Eliminate the parts of the business that are not as fruitful. Just take them right out of the deck!

Okay...so we know WHAT we want to accomplish. We are fully convinced that doing an open house in this area is really important in the execution of our plan. We are also diligent in ensuring that we leverage and maximize our EMT. (Energy, Money and Time). Right? Because a 4X Agent understands the power of multiplication. A 4X Agent operates with intention. You have established the market that you want to go after. You have decided on the target area of homes that you want to market.

You have found a way to do an open house. You know you have the right listing because you know what a "right listing" is. In the next chapter, we are going to go over the marketing sequence leading up to the open house to create a great chance of success. We are going to stack the cards in our favor. The week prior to the open house is critical to the success that you will achieve.

MARKETING STRATEGIES LEADING UP TO THE OPEN HOUSE

Is your objective clear? Are you ready to move forward confidently? When you contact FSBOs and Expired listings and you are talking to your peers in your office to get an open house booked, you need to have do have clear objectives. In staging an open house, you want to attract leads and plant seeds for more leads later. It's as simple as that. You want to meet the top two criteria that buyers and sellers say is most important to them. Develop a good reputation as someone who is valuable, honest, up-to-date and a hard-working, someone who knows their community and neighbourhood well. If you work diligently and take all the necessary steps, you will find that these things will happen automatically and organically.

Approach a mortgage broker or lender and ask them out for lunch. If you have a mortgage person to contact, ask them if they would like to attend your open house with you. They will get a chance to be the first contact at the open house, ensuring that people fill out the sign-in forms. If they can include your home in a feature sheet, that would be great. The sheet should provide three different calculations for mortgage scenarios. I would suggest something like, two high ratio scenarios and then one scenario with 25% down payment or equity, depending on the target market that you believe you are attracting.

Think about the three finance scenarios you may come across. Additionally, the feature sheet should speak to the regular closing costs that a buyer would incur in a fairly normal transaction. It should also deal with details such as insurance, legal fees, inspection fees, appraisal costs and tax adjustments, This is especially important if your target market is made up of a lot of first-or second-time buyers. I find that these clients will keep this information longer and use it in their private discussions afterwards. That form should also be co-branded with your mortgage professional so that you are positioned as a team.

The Power of Edification

Another aspect of this arrangement is to talk about *edification*. Edification is a powerful thing when done properly. When speaking to the people who are attending the open house, in later meetings, or in meetings with people you have both referred, it is so important to remember to edify each other. When I speak to people about my team, I want them to know that everyone on my team is amazing! They are attentive. They are organized. They are accountable. They are patient and understanding. They work hard to get the best possible result for people. This is the language that I use. The truth is, if they don't have all these positive qualities, they are off the team. Simple as that. They have to live up to those standards and each team member needs to know that. And you should be living up to those standards, too. On the other hand, your team members should also be edifying *you,* as well, naming some of the same attributes that people in the buyer target market will want to know about.

Remember the nine facets of the 4X Agent and the 4X Manifesto? You DO and you ARE—right? Remember to do this consciously at first; it will become a habit later. This is very important to your long-term success.

Okay, let's move on to the marketing progression of the open house. We have allowed ourselves enough lead time to properly market the event open house. Here is the sequence of events on the week prior to the weekend of the open house. Let's say you have booked the open house for Saturday from 2-4pm for the public, and 1-2pm for the neighbors to pop by.

Here is an example of the week leading up to the open house:

Monday: Shoot video – install sign to promote the weekend

Prior to the open house, go to the property and shoot a little preliminary 30-second video to post on social media. Do a quick and easy edit on it. If you have a website, post the video on there. You are going to blast it out, on multiple social media platforms, and make sure you send it to the seller and tag them, so that they share it. If your office has social media pages, then get them to share it as well. If you are doing the open house for another agent, make sure that they share it and promote the open house as well on their social media. Don't leave anything to chance.

The video content should be something very simple. Something like...

"Hey everybody! This is .... from .... realty. Just taking a moment to tell you about this awesome house located on .... Street and I am really excited about it...If you are looking for a house with a large, fenced yard, double garage, 3 bedrooms and a den in a great subdivision, come

on by on Saturday between 2-4pm and I will be there. If you know of anybody looking for something like this, please share the video and let them know about it. This is ....from ....Realty working hard in the Morningside Park area of Salem, Oregon. I love this neighbourhood for so many reasons...I hope to get a chance to tell you all about it this Saturday from 2 to 4...see you then!"

This is just one idea for a video. It's quick and to the point. Make sure to move the camera around a bit to show off the street. Show the front of the house. Show the neighboring homes. Remind them about the date and time of the open house—twice. Share a few quick details about the house to help people know a little bit more about it. Some neighbours may see you doing this. This is a good thing. Also, if you can get a sign on an H frame, please do so; just a simple chloroplast sign to put on the front lawn. The sign doesn't have to have your name on it, all it has to say is **OPEN HOUSE – THIS SATURDAY 2-4PM.** Having toppers for your own listings is a powerful form of branding and marketing. If you have metal signs, the toppers can be magnetic and simply stick to your sign. It just reinforces once again that you are working. Imagine if you had four open houses all in the same neighborhood, with your signs all over the front lawns showing all your open houses. This is powerful stuff. These signs are "speaking" to your neighbourhood all week. When the buyers do a little drive-by, they see the sign. Buyers drive-by all the time and we aren't necessarily aware when it happens. My opinion, is, you need to have a sign working for you. I would get a bunch of them made. They are very inexpensive marketing that is speaking to the target market that you want. I would get two signs made for each time slot for both Saturdays and Sundays. For example: 1-3pm on one, 12-2pm on another, 2-4pm on one, and 1-4pm on another.

The last thing you can do, while you are at the home, is to drop off the brochure, "How to get ready for an open house" to the seller [www.4Xformula.com/attractbook]. This is a gentle nudge to the seller to do their part in preparing for the open house. You are working hard to make sure that there is good attendance and exposure. Their job is to ensure that the home is ready and looking its best for the event.

Tuesday: Send out video – enter into MLS open house info

Video should be edited now and ready to send it to the seller to share; make them see how hard you have been working. If you can access the video in your MLS, go in there and make sure that the open house is also set up in the MLS system. If you have met anyone in an open house recently from the neighbourhood, send the video to their email as an invitation. If your local real estate organizations have some specific social media pages that you can post on, then make sure to do so. In the comments, reach out to buyers even if their agents won't be able to attend, make it clear that their agent's commission will be honored. **Wednesday: Get marketing materials ready – boost Facebook and Instagram post for FOUR days**.

Work on the invite for the neighbourhood. Keep it simple but professional. In the wording, tell them why you love the neighbourhood. You have scheduled the open house for the public from 2-4pm but make it very clear that there is a special invitation for neighbours to come and view the home and enjoy some snacks from 1-2pm. Boost the video from Wednesday for four days, to target area demographic. Don't hesitate to spend $10 on Facebook and Instagram ads. If your Facebook and Instagram aren't set up as a business page yet, then don't worry about it. We can tackle that another time.

Thursday: <u>Hand Deliver Invites and Open House promo</u>.

Two days before the open house is a good time to notify the surrounding neighbours of the upcoming event. Aim to hit 100 to 200 homes but, at the very least, notify the surrounding 20 homes. The "Tell 20" rule is non-negotiable. Knock on the doors of the 20 nearest homes as a personal invitation; if they don't answer, leave the invite in the crack of the front door. [By the way, an invitation is not a "solicitation" in my opinion; make sure the people in your neighbourhood have the same attitude.]

If someone answers the door, try using very simple script...

*"Hi, I'm.......................... from .... Realty and I am just letting you know about an open house that I am doing on Saturday. "[*Lean in, use a lower voice, like it's a secret*]... "I wanted to personally invite you to a showing just for neighbours from 1-2pm. I will have some snacks and refreshments there. Do you think that you can make it by? Either way, I would love the opportunity to meet you and anyone else you bring by...Can't* make it?...*Okay, no problem... hey, I'll leave this invite with you anyway and if you know of anyone looking for a home like theirs, would you do me a favor and just send them on over. I'm just doing the best I can for [first names of sellers] to find the right buyer for their home. By the way, tell me...what do you love best about this neighbourhood?"*

At this point, LISTEN...and use FORM. Maybe this leads to a conversation. Don't force it. But something may be uncovered here. If so, figure out something that you can do for them and then do it. Make an offer and see if they accept. "*Well, it was great meeting you. I wish you all the best. Take care and have a great night/day/evening/afternoon."*

Leave a good impression. You never know. That was seed planting. If it was your listing, you would have already dropped off a "**Just LISTED Flyer**" and this is now the second time they are getting something from you. This may be the first time actually meeting you. This is just the start. More on that later in the course.

Friday: Do another video.

This time, focus on the neighbourhood. Address the character and the lifestyle of this area. Mention parks, schools, amenities, recreation facilities, any facility that someone in the neighbourhood has told you about. If you are doing a draw for a prize of some sort, then this is a good time to talk about that, too. It doesn't have to be a long video; 30 seconds to less than a minute, tops. Send it to the seller to post and post it all over the place yourself, just like before. If you have time, and there are more neighbours to inform about the open house tomorrow, then get out there and tell more people. Make sure you have dropped off flyers and door-knocked all of the FSBOs and the Recent Expireds in the area, for sure. Even if their addresses are a little bit out of the way, invite them. If you met anyone in any prior open houses who filled out an open house "sign in" form, then give them a call to personally invite them, too.

SATURDAY: Set up the open house.

This is the big day! Begin set up at least one hour before the event. Set up signs from the farthest distance you plan to mark and then work your way back to the home. Make sure you have lots of signs. If you're just starting out, do your best. But I would like to see a minimum of 10 to 20 signs, if you can. Get a flag for the front of the house. Put signs on every corner that has access to the house. Place signs on the main roads and then multiple signs leading up to the house. People need to think that there is a carnival happening somewhere in their subdivision! Tie balloons or flags on all the major signs. However, if you are poking any signs in the ground instead of using sandwich boards, make sure to respect another person's private property. I would suggest that you kindly knock on their door to make sure it is okay to do that. Think of it as another contact opportunity and another way to stand out from the rest who never take the time to ask. If they aren't home, leave a card in the door and carry on with your sign placement. You tried. If they call you, you can tell them the reason you left your card. Who knows, it may open up an opportunity. How many other agents are doing that? Not many.

Remember this is your neighbourhood. These are your target market people. Building reputation is extremely important. Remember that? Reputation is the top criteria for both buyers and sellers. Reputation.

Here is another stat we need to be aware of: 5% of success with clients that we meet for the first time occurs from the first contact. Just 5%. This is where a lot of real estate agents fail. Your sole purpose for expending all of this time, energy, creativity and money is simply to meet people. It's just the start.

Here is another stat: Your chances increase dramatically to a 95% success rate with five or more follow-up contact points. We have built in a few just in the lead-up to the open house. We have created two to three contact touches by reaching out to the FSBOs and Expireds. We are meeting the neighbours and creating opportunities to have conversations with them in the neighbourhood where they are comfortable. We give them home field advantage, right?

But after we meet them, how do we create ways to contact them again? Once someone attends an open house and meets you and your mortgage partner, do we know how to stay in touch with them? We do so by purposefully focusing on them, by finding ways to reach out to them, using all types of methods and mediums: face to face, social media, paper, signage, letters and notes, phone calls.

In just one month, you have made your presence known! You are creating relevance. You are building reputation. You are gaining knowledge and understanding. You are gaining confidence. You are becoming the master of your target market. You are getting to know people you have never met before. You are expanding your sphere of influence. Getting out of your little box, you are increasing your odds. You are stacking the cards in your favor. You are quickly becoming the *Neighbourhood Specialist.*

Later on in the book we will cover the rest of the activities that you will do to become the absolute best neighbourhood specialist. You will own this neighbourhood, and literally become its go-to person. The top-of-mind professional for this neighborhood. The wheels are turning now. Momentum is gearing up! This is the ultimate goal, and this will pay you for decades. Next, we are going to cover, the 7 Stages of Contact when you meet someone at an Open House.

Go and download the Open House checklist at www.4Xformula.com/attractbook.

THE SEVEN STAGES OF CONTACT

Okay, let's recap. We have spent time talking about the overall plan for our business building and how important the open house is to the 4X Formula game plan. We have discussed the preliminary work required to give you the best chance of meeting your target market. You know who your target market is. You have learned about how to make great conversation.

So...now it's showtime. You are all set up. The marketing has been done. You have met people who live in the neighborhood. You have put up the signs. The house is looking great. With the Open House Checklist in hand, you are prepared to handle every single type of situation that can arise. You are ready to welcome people into the home.

Your goal is to meet people, leave a positive impression and plant seeds for future business. At the same time, you are looking for those one or two potential clients who are ready to buy or sell now and need your help. Our mission is clear, right? Meeting people, building rapport, and then instilling trust: This is what we do as real estate agents. Developing a solid understanding of how relationships work in an open house setting is critical to succeeding in the real estate business. If you "lock in" just one buyer per weekend, you can make over $100,000 per year just from the buyer leads you meet from open houses! That is exciting! Then apply the 4X Formula to those leads and you are on your way to building a fantastic business.

Today we are going to cover the Seven Stages of Contact with people who attend your open houses. It is important to recognize that there are stages that you progress through when people attend your open houses. Everyone has a different expectation when they walk through the door. Most people are still wary of being "sold." They carry with them that instinctive reaction to say, "just looking," the same way you do when you walk into a clothing store. I am sure you relate. When you walk into a clothing store and the "welcome person" says "How are you today...is there anything that I can help you with?" Your instinctive answer is "Just looking." There are layers of protectiveness that you need to work your way through. Some people have more layers than others.

With that in mind, I have broken everything down into the Seven Stages of Contact. Accept the fact that you aren't going to make it to stage seven with everyone who attends an open house. But if you approach it according to the plan that we set out in Part Two of Master of the Open House, then it is just about guaranteed that you'll get to Stage Seven. According to our mission, that is all you need.

Okay, let's kick in on this. But before we move on into the Seven Stages of Contact, I want you to keep in mind that any movement to another stage is where we apply the concepts in Mindset Mastery, the Art of the Conversation and utilizing FORM...with clear intention. Advancing to each stage is a mini-success. You will get better and better at this every time you practice it, and be able to mentally measure your success, based on your understanding of these seven stages.

1st Stage: Welcome.

To set the tone, I always welcome people in various ways when they enter the open house. I say something to ease the tension and minimize their fear that I might try to sell them something. I am just a person who is welcoming them into a home. I am simply the host. The welcome should vary slightly from person to person, because other people just entering may hear me welcome the next person, so it shouldn't be exactly the same each time. For some script ideas to start you out, go to www.4Xformula.com/attractbook. Eventually, you will come up with some sentences that fit your personality. If you have been sitting on the couch...get up. Walk towards the door but softly. Keep it subtle but make sure that you display to the people entering that they are important, and that you are ready to help them. Your body language should feel casual and non-threatening.

After "the welcome," you then want to get everyone into chit-chat mode. Make it easy for them. I suggest picking topics that are simple, and comfortable. Talk about the weather or traffic or how busy your open house is; these are all "common ground" topics that act like ice-breakers. They will help you gauge people's personality types and help you determine how thick their barriers are. That is Stage One.

The Second Stage: The sign-in sheet.

How you approach this stage is up to you, but I would encourage you to get into a habit of requiring people to sign in at an open house. (I have included some nice "sign-in" sheets at www.4Xformula.com/attractbook.) The sign-in sheets we provide give people an option to sign in and give you authority to contact them later. Some people will simply agree with your request and sign in. They will fill it out completely and smile and move on.

But keep in mind, there are some people who will NOT sign, no matter what. Let's take a moment to talk about this.

Think of it this way: This is somebody's personal home. They have personal belongings here. The sellers are allowing people to walk around, in their home. They have a right to require you to enforce the sign-in form. Instead of making it a "contact form" for YOU, think of it as a record-keeping document for the seller, for security purposes. See the difference? It's not you who requires the sign-in, it's the seller. You are just doing your job. Try this:

"Can I please have one of you fill out the form, for the seller please? Thanks a lot. They have asked that I get all attendees to sign in, for security reasons."

If people don't want to fill it out and seem pretty firm on this, alter your request:

"I need you to simply put your names on there...don't worry about the rest of the contact info. Sound fair?"

If they absolutely refuse, this is where you decide how much you want to enforce this. But if you want to stay firm on this, try walking them through a worst-case scenario:

"Well, I have this policy for this reason. Picture this if you will: Something gets broken, or something goes missing or someone comes back later, after casing the place, and, a theft occurs, and I have to talk to the police about it. I would be pretty embarrassed if I was not able to show that I at least attempted to get the names of the people who walked through the home. If you are worried about me bothering you after the open house, then don't put your contact information on there, okay? Just your names. That's totally fine. Thank you for understanding."

And then stand there and be silent. They will at least put their names down. They might be fake names. That's okay. Hopefully, you will have an opportunity to earn the right to get their real contact information later as you work through some more layers. This is not the only chance you will get to earn their trust, in my opinion. Keep in mind that, if this *is* the only time, then they are simply not the one that you are looking for today, anyway. Right? Accept that. It's okay.

Lastly, think about using a "draw." People like to win things; give them that reason to sign-in, to enter the "draw." But be careful about this. There are situations where a draw is a great idea. But I don't want you to rely on that to get names or leads. You shouldn't have to rely on *bait* to get people to fill out a form in an open house. I want you to be able to rely on your ability to progress through the stages of contact to create a lead...a real lead. And then an actual contact. I like to focus on quality rather than quantity.

Okay. On to Stage 3. Easy-to-answer questions.

Here is the thought process: A person has made a personal choice to come to your open house. From all of the signage and marketing that has taken place, they know that a real estate representative will be there. They know the house is for sale. This is not a secret. They realize you have a job to do. Some of these people are actually hoping that you are the type of real estate professional who is more likely to be sitting on the couch watching the football game and won't even get off the couch to talk to them. They want to come in, see the home, and get out as fast as possible. On the other hand, there are others who have nothing else to do on a Saturday or Sunday afternoon and they love checking out open houses. It's a hobby of theirs. They quite possibly may be making a move in a couple years but there is absolutely no sense of urgency at all. They are happy to chat and tell you all about themselves but they're not going to do anything in the near future and, a lot of times, they are not loyal to any particular real estate agent. Then there are the people who are thinking very seriously about making a move. It may be their first time, out and about, looking at homes. They are a little wary. They may even seem a little shifty.

They are the "just looking" people but they *do* actually want to learn about the neighbourhood. They might even want to see this home to see if it would actually work for their family. They are in the research stage. *These* are the people you are looking for, your target. You're going to want to be very helpful to anyone in this phase. They are your perfect candidates.

You are now in Stage Three. These questions are all about getting some clues. Give them information and allow them freedom to feel relaxed in this space. They need to feel that it is okay to be here, and they want to feel comfortable. You need to give them a chance to fall in love with the house, or to analyze it or discuss it freely. This is really important. Give them space but, first, ask a few questions to establish which type of open house attendees they are. Establish if they have a purpose and are actively looking for homes. If it's obvious right away, don't pounce on them. Let them get climatized first. Our goal is now to gauge whether they are truly interested in making a move, or just purely curious.

Plant a seed here. That's all. If they are in the target group, the next thing we want to establish is whether they are local or from out of town. This is important for later. But that's it for now. You are only in Stage Three. Let them look at the home, because it will be the tool for the next stage. I have given you a bunch of suggestions for questions that you can ask at www.4Xformula.com/attractbook, but the overall intention here is to peel off the first layer and see if this is someone worth pursuing a little deeper. Are these people part of the 40%? Are they warming up? Look and listen for clues. Okay?

Alright, next is the 4th Stage. <u>Talk about the house.</u>

Think about this for a second. We are only a few minutes into the process. These first few stages are about discovery. But they are also part of a process that shows that you are a competent professional who is in control. Now, we just want to bring it all back to the house itself. This is more comfortable for the viewer. Tell them a few things about the home that are not necessarily obvious at first glance, or maybe some specific things that we want them to notice as they walk through. You've already gotten through the first uncomfortable stage, the welcome, the sign-in, the introductions. Remember, the people arrived to look at the home, and don't want to be bombarded and peppered with questions. Most people need some space at this point, but you still want to show them that you are there to do a job for your seller. You are a professional. You are in control. You operate with intention. You are organized and prepared. The attitude here is kind of like this: You are obtaining permission, but you are going to tell them anyway, because it is important.

It might seem obvious but the truth is, we have to assume that they are there to learn about the home. If you are very professional, informative, and friendly, it adjusts their expectation. If they are not accustomed to this, this is actually a good thing. This is where you will stand out. If they are a "nosy neighbour" — great — they are witnessing how you operate. They can't help but feel that you are there "working" for your seller. You are planting a seed here.

Show who you are working for. Try saying things like this: *"The seller asked me to mention a few things about this house and then I'll let you go..."* Focus on a few really neat features in the home. This is where your enthusiasm should expand. Your excitement will be infectious: *"There are a couple really cool features about this house...do you mind if I take a moment to tell you about a few things first? And then I'll let you wander around...sound okay?"* Simply ask permission, and show you take your job seriously: *"Before I let you wander through the home, do you mind, if I take a quick moment and do my job for the seller? I just want to let you know about a few things that you may or may not notice as you walk through the home..."* This is a good time to tell them about any updates, any replaced items (such as furnaces, hot water heaters, roofs, plumbing, etc.) or any renovations or upgrades to electrical, plumbing or drainage. Hand them your well-designed feature sheet for the home. On the counter you will have more information which may spark a conversation or bring up some questions or queries. This is good. Listen and let them talk. Ask questions that give them more time to talk. Listen and learn. Then encourage them to wander around the home. Make it obvious that you are now going to leave them alone. After they have had some time to walk around, you are looking for an opening to get into a deeper discussion with them, to see if they are the people that you might be able to "lock in."

Through stages one to four, you have narrowed things down and have discerned if your target clients meet the criteria. If they meet a lot of the criteria, but it seems that they are not going to be making a move for a few months then segue into stage five, with the understanding that you are working towards future business. If there is someone in the open house that is hot and ready to buy, and you have a chance to get into a deeper discussion with that person or group, then you need to focus on that. Ultimately, you want to achieve both, while at the same time planting seeds with neighbors for future listings.

Let's pause for a second here.

Do you see what is happening? I think it is important to acknowledge at this stage how everything is culminating. This is the 4X formula at work. This is how you harness the power of multiplication. This is how you 4X your business. I know that not everyone who walks through that door is in a position to buy today. I know that I am not going to be the sole influencer and power source who causes them to buy a home when they are not ready to do so. I am not the master salesperson who will convince these people to do something that is not in their best interests. This is never going to happen. To operate with that level of thinking is horrendously wrong. Do you agree?

Take that pressure off yourself. Very rarely do people write offers on their first visit to a home. Car salesmen worry about people leaving their car lot and going across the road to buy somewhere else, so they are always working on closing. We are not closers. Believe it or not, we will actually close more deals by remembering what our role truly is: We help people improve their lifestyles. We help people maximize their investments. We help people make great family decisions. We help people find the perfect fit that works best for them. We have access to all of the products. Is there a house for every single type of buyer out there? YES. There is. It's out there. The whole MLS system is our inventory. Our job is to use the resources that are at hand to assist these people in a major life event. They will eventually work with somebody. There are over two million real estate agents out there. Our competition is the Top 20%. There are 400,000 people out there doing pretty good business. If it's not you, it's one of them for sure.

So, is that somebody going to be you, today, tomorrow or a year from now? Will it be YOU? Remember that statistic? 75% of buyers and sellers decided to work with the first agent they came into contact with. Remember that? So, with that in mind, what can we control? What is in our power? What influence can we have?

In simple terms, we can prove to everyone we come into contact with that we are someone who can be of value to them, either now, or sometime in the near future. People want the 4X Agent. They do. They want someone in their corner who is organized, accountable and trustworthy. Someone who is a consummate professional. Someone who operates with intention and builds relationships. Someone who is prepared, consistent and in control. This is who they want.

In addition to that, a 4X Agent is someone who maximizes their time. All of that time that you are spending on your open house event is to build your business. This is your storefront on that day! So be careful not to discard and sacrifice future business for the one lead that is going to satisfy TODAY only.

Real estate is a delicate dance. That's why it is important to be prepared and have materials at the open house to give to people as a take-away for various situations. If someone is interested in this home but working with another agent then there is a package for that. Figure out how to make it easy for them to buy. Eliminate friction. Let's get that house sold. If someone is not interested in the home but maybe thinking about selling in the near future, then there is a package or handout for that, too, about how you market homes. If someone is in the research stage then there is a package for that: similar homes you may want to show them, a couple of days from now. Be prepared for every opportunity.

And, really...just about every person who walks through that open house door is an opportunity. How can you help them? How can you be of value? Anticipate those opportunities. Anticipate what they are going to want before they ask. Anticipate the questions and have the answers. You are prepared. You are organized. You are intentional. You maximize your time. In one open house, you can meet a potential seller, a future buyer who might also need to sell something, and a "right now" buyer who needs your expertise. **That is four deals right there, from one open house**! When that person eventually lists their home with you, there are another four deals. See how it all comes together? Plant the seeds. Be that person they are looking for. You can literally build up a great business from working open houses properly.

Now we are going to move into the 5th Stage. We have welcomed them to the home, addressed the signing-in portion of the visit, asked some fairly surface-type, non-threatening, questions. We have given them handouts and verbal information and let them wander through the home. Throughout this process, we are arranging these people into categories. That is what is happening all the time in your mind. Remember the NOW, NEVER, LATER thing I was talking about before? This is what you are doing mentally. Some people have come and gone. Some people have figured out how to escape without having to speak to you anymore. Some people are in a hurry. Some people are working with another agent and wanted to do a little preview on their own. That is *all fine*. This is what happens at an open house. Your key mission for the seller is that you are exposing the home to many people. The more people you expose the home, the better chance of selling the home. But at the same time, the more people who come through that door, the more chances you have to meet your target buyer or next seller, someone who needs your help today, tomorrow or some day in the future.

Okay, we are now working our way to Stage Five. This is a subtle transition because, depending on what is happening with the conversation or the walk-through tour, you may be gently entering into that stage without even knowing it.

5th Stage: Let them go but focus on attempting to get some "F.O.R.M. time."

Talk about the home, but ask questions to learn more about them—move into F.O.R.M.

Every real estate professional has a different style here, so do what is comfortable for you; but be intentional. The style of the house plan influences this as well. Do you follow them around? Do you hover in the vicinity? Are there some things about the rooms they should see? Do you give them space and listen for reactions? Do you stay on the main floor and let them walk around by themselves on the other floors?

I don't believe there is any one hard and fast rule as to how you host an open house. Each situation influences how you manage each event, such as: *This is the first open house following the listing launch.* This one would be crafted a little differently, right? Or maybe the open house is well attended and you have multiple groups that need to be welcomed. Some sellers only allow one group through at a time. Others let everyone in and allow them to bump into each other. You may be alone at this open house. If you are by yourself this time, it will dictate how you approach your plan. It happens.

The style of the home can also influence your plan. It might be a one-level or a three- or four-level home. It is best, if you have another real estate or a mortgage professional with you to help with the first couple of stages. This can also dictate how you deal with the sign-in forms and the "walk throughs." Another complication is if the listing is in a condo building that has additional security. You may need to have someone in the entrance to bring people upstairs. That can pose another challenge. The point here is to have a plan, but be flexible with it.

The execution of the plan is focused on making sure that these three items are taken care of properly:

1. The sign-in sheets
2. Ensuring people are getting the information on the home
3. Meeting people and having as many discussions as possible.

When you meet people, always be listening for clues and don't forget to pay special attention to the people who seem to be more apt to listening and giving feedback. These people have fewer layers. More often than not, this is because they are actively looking for a home. Focus on these people and get to the 5th Stage and beyond, if possible. Remember you are looking for one person for sure, and two if you can, who are ready to buy. Hot buyers. If you haven't already found one, by now, you need to determine if they are working with another agent or not. Maybe they have viewed some homes with someone but don't feel obligated to that person. Don't press on this. If they have grown to like you, they will let you know if they are open to working with you. It will come out in the conversation in some way. However, the proper etiquette is to ask. They will respect either one of these questions:

"Has anyone been helping you out so far?"

"Have you been working with an agent to help you find the perfect home?"

"Who is your buyer's agent?"

"Have you chosen a professional to help you yet?"

This is really important**:** If they make it clear that they are working with another agent and are interested in the home, give them a full information packet. Talk up the home, talk up the neighbourhood and make sure that they know about all of the features and benefits. Ask them for their real estate agent information and promise them that you will get an information package to that person, in order to help expedite things. If they are agreeable, then you know they are quite interested; If they seem hesitant, then they may not be very interested in the home. Either way, the extra effort is worth it. If they feel that they have to look at more homes, there is a good chance they will come back to your listing later. You just never know.

Be easy to work with and respectful of the client/agent relationship. This humanizes the process and makes it hard for them to think of you as an adversary when negotiations start. This is not a factor that a lot of real estate agents consider, but is important. Do your best job for the seller. Then, look for the next buyer to focus on. Now, if they are open to working with someone and they are not committed to someone else, then its game on! Great. This could be the one. If so, watch their body language. Body language doesn't lie. Be conscious of that.

Now, remember that nine times out of ten, this is not going to be the home for them. There will be something that they don't like. You can tell if someone is genuinely interested in the home for themselves and are starting to imagine themselves living there, or if they're not. If you determine that they are someone who is a buyer—a "right now" buyer—but this isn't the home for them, move into a mode of "locking them in." Now you need information so you can figure out how to help them. That's it. You may want to ease the tension here as well. It's likely that they aren't necessarily ready to show any vulnerability yet. You will have to earn it. If you can convince them that you are someone they can trust, and that you are capable—someone who is in their corner.... you will be working with these people and helping them find a home.

This is where your conversation skills come into play, where *The Art of Conversation* is really important. Utilize F.O.R.M. to gather valuable intel. Look for signs. Listen for clues. Learn about them. Be open to opportunity. How can you help? How can you be useful? How can you become a person of value for these people? F. O. R.M: Family... Occupation ...Recreation...Message. Always ask questions that relate to these areas; move the conversation to a more comfortable state. This is where you are 'humanizing' the visit. Just a few people getting to know each other. If possible, try to engage in a deeper conversation, preferably in an area of the home that appeals to the buyer's emotions. If the house has a nice view, maybe have the conversation on the deck or at a large window, so they are looking at a panorama. If the kitchen is amazing, get in position there, or maybe in a cozy and comfortable living room. Talking about their dreams in the basement, in the furnace room or in the garage is not an optimum experience, normally.

If you have reached this moment, you are entering the next stage.

The 6th Stage: Get to the message and obtain permission.

You have now reached a point in the process where some crucial questions will be raised. Your queries are now getting more direct but as long as you have spent enough time getting to know the clients, it will be comfortable enough to ask them. If you are still chatting with these people and gaining a clearer understanding of their goals, you have earned their trust and broken through most of the barriers. Now is the time to summarize what you have learned and show them that you can take control of the situation and simplify the process for them. Normally, people in this situation want someone to take control and bring clarity to the process. Show them the path.

At this point, I would grab the sign-in sheet and start making notes on the back. In your summary, make it clear that you have heard what is important to them. You might want to ask more questions, but it's also important at this stage to prove to them that you are listening, and that you are gaining a clearer understanding of their specific needs. Where are they in the process? What challenges they are facing? What other aspects of the process need clarification? What type of home works best for them? What are they currently lacking and what do they want now? What is their budget? What don't they know and how can you help them know it? More Importantly, what is their timeline? What is their motivation? What hurdles need to be overcome? Who can you introduce them to, in order to help expedite things? What aspects of the location are important to them? What stage of life are they at? What changes are taking place in their life that is causing them to make a change? For some other questions, check out www.4Xformula.com/attractbook.

Take time to read over the Seven Stages of Contact and get to know the questions and the different phrasing styles. You will find different ways to pose these questions, different ways that work with your style and personality, but I just wanted to give you something to help you get there. So, how do we summarize and work our way into asking for the business?

Here is an example of using a statement that leads into more questions. But at the same time, I am summarizing, and asking permission to work my way to Stage Seven:

"So, Bob and Andrea, it seems to me that you are in the early stages of looking for another home, am I right? And this home here, doesn't really suit your needs. You need at least one more bedroom and you prefer the master bedroom on the main floor. Is that correct? Also, I think that I heard Bob mention that, if you had room for the RV beside the home, that would be great, right? Your current home over on ....street, is in a great area, and I know there are buyers for that type of home, but you said you want to spend a little time getting it ready to market in the spring. I think that is smart. If you think that it might help, I could come over and assess things so that you don't spend money on things that won't really get you the maximum amount of money. I might have a few suggestions that are less costly that can really impact the sell-ability of you home. We can do that if you like...would you find that helpful?"

Go into booking a time with them. Do you see what is happening? In this scenario, I am summarizing and checking in, as I go. This is a very real circumstance that you may run across. You are a valuable resource. Can you save them some money? Yes, you can. As I check in, they are agreeing with me and nodding their heads with me as I am checking in. I am solidifying our relationship. I have summarized their plan and, at the same time, made them feel intelligent because I have pointed out how clear it is to me that they have put some thought into this. I don't want to challenge them at this point. A lot of real estate trainers will try to overcome "the waiting to sell" objection in this conversation. I don't believe this is the right time. Instead, your goal is to get a chance to visit them at their home and offer some suggestions and build more value into the relationship.

You then graduate from meeting them in an open house to visiting them in their home. You become more invested in each other. Once you visit with them and tour their home, make sure to think about how to serve them best. It may be a fact that they don't need to do anything to the home to get it ready, and that now, truly, is the best time to sell. That is a very real possibility, but it will be much more believable after you have invested some time assessing the situation. Not only that, if selling the house is the end result, you will most likely have come to that conclusion together anyway.

You want them to trust your advice. You want them to feel that your advice is in their best interest and not yours. If you challenge them the first time that you meet them, there is no way that they can trust that you are operating in their best interest. You haven't earned that right yet.

I hope that this makes sense because a 4X Agent builds relationships. This is relationship building. Something could change in their lives the day after tomorrow and this whole process could go onto the backburner. If you have built a relationship with them, then there is a good chance that they will refer business to you, and you will absolutely do business with them, when the time is right...as long as you have taken the time to build a relationship, first. That is 4X'ing your business! This happens to me all the time. A 4X Agent receives referrals too, right?

7th Stage: – <u>You earn the right to be THEIR real estate representative.</u>

You are their confidante, and they are your client. This is now a relationship. You are now part of one another's lives. You are a positive influence in their sphere. You are someone that they trust. You are their advisor in all things real estate related and more. Do a great job for these people, nurture the opportunity for referrals, and you are on your way to 4Xing your business. Two per listing: That's all you need! Congratulations! This is the conclusion to Master of the Open House. Please visit www.4Xformula.com/attract-book for more information on how to finesse open houses.

NEIGHBOURHOOD SPECIALIST

Everything is all coming together now.

All of the prior lessons have brought us to this point, everything you have learned and everything you have applied, and all of the action steps that you have taken. Everything has been for a very specific purpose. If you have been doing your homework—and applying the steps and intentionally focusing your efforts according to the plan that we have laid out—then you will be experiencing some mini-successes and maybe some great and fantastic successes, too! You are gaining more confidence as you have been implementing the tools that I have created for you. This is your new life. This is what you do now. You are becoming a real estate professional who is building a great reputation and becoming a fixture in your neighbourhood. Remember the two main criteria that buyers and sellers look for are "reputation" and "knowledge of the area." So, with that in mind, let's move into the strategies that are going to solidify this for you.

You have identified your target market. You have identified the product type. You have drilled down to a neighbourhood that dominates that market. All of the FSBOs that are for sale right now know who you are. You have offered value to them, viewed their homes, spoken to them on the phone, and dropped off information and letters for them. You have met them in person and invited them to open houses that you are organizing. You are letting them know when you list a home and when you sell a home. You have viewed every listing in the neighbourhood and in every other neighbourhood that meets the target that you are after. You know what is going on. You have contacted all the Expired listings and they know who you are. You aren't simply a picture on a postcard mail-out that they received once and then threw away. You are a person who has communicated value to them.

That's the key right there...you are a person to them now.

Planting Seeds

You have started planting seeds in the neighbourhood, with the neighbours who may be thinking about buying and selling in the future. Some of them might have witnessed you making a video outside the home, or saw you putting up signs, or saw you walking the neighbourhood delivering invitations. You are more than just some "salesy" person now.

You are becoming 'Top of Mind.' You are gaining mindshare. You are meeting buyers who are part of the target market at your well-planned and well-marketed open house events. You are planting seeds there, too. Some people have taken you up on your offer to help them with buying or selling and you are busy helping them. That is awesome and very exciting. We know the National Association of Real Estate stats and we are embarking on the activities that give us the best chance of success, based on what the general public is telling us they want.

In a relatively short period of time, you have made an impact in the neighbourhood. You started something and you are quickly becoming recognizable. You know people now who you did not know two or three weeks ago. You are adding people to your Leads List. You are filling out contact cards. You are building your database while becoming an active member of this neighbourhood. The key word here is **active**.

Let's take a moment to be patently clear on what the purpose of ATTRACT is and why it is so important. There are three factors that create certainty and comfort in the real estate business.

The 3 Cs of Success

Consistency — Conversion Rates — and Currency

1. **Consistency:** Consistency in income is created from consistency in activity. You are getting paid today from the activity that you performed 90 days ago. If that is 0, then the activities were not producing any consistency. I have been paid a commission cheque – at least 1 – but very seldom just 1 – and sometimes as much as 20 commission cheques in a month for over 18 years and counting. That is because I am consistent with my activity, even when I was doing it wrong.
2. **Conversion Rates:** Your ability to Convert will increase with consistent activity. Remember: CONVERSATION -> CONVERSION -> to LEAD -> TO CONTACT -> TO CONTRACT – All of your activity is meant to create more conversations.
3. **Currency:** Increasing your $/hour is in direct correlation to your Consistency and your ability to Convert LEADS to CONTRACTs and then create lifelong CLIENTS who refer business to you to increase your ability to convert which increases your Currency exponentially.

Consistency

The ultimate real estate business has multiple cheques paying out in a month—every month. Would it give you comfort and certainty to have future deals filling up the months to come? Remember when we were talking about focusing on what you want, instead of what you are afraid of?

When I was golfing at the Golden Eagle, I was focusing on the water—the outcome I didn't want. Where did the ball end up? In the water, right? I knew how to hit a ball. I knew how to swing. I knew where I wanted to end up, but I wasn't really focusing on that. I was focusing on the water instead of the green grass, the fairway.

Do you want consistent commission cheques every month? Then focus on **that** and do what is taught here and you will have it. The key to creating consistency in your business is the ability to manage your leads, contacts and strategic alliances all at the same time. Each "seed" you plant will sprout at a different times, but you have to water and fertilize those seeds/leads all the time. Even when you are benefiting from the "low hanging fruit" and the seeds are all coming to fruition, you have to be nurturing referrals, strategic alliances, past clients, future buyers and sellers, all at the same time. This is constant. Leads never, ever dry up, if you operate this way. Consistent effort, every day, will guarantee consistent income.

Conversion Rates

What are normal conversion rates? I use the Ten and Two Rule. If an agent is door-knocking, the ratio is about 300 and 2. Not great— that's why I don't do door-knocking and never have. If you are going to knock on someone's door, you better be providing some sort of value for that person, or it is an absolute waste of time. When you meet people who are excited to meet you, do you think you can increase your conversion rates? I'm talking about people who were referred to you by other happy clients. People who are in your neighborhood and decided six months ago that when they were ready to make a move, that they were going to contact you. You get much better conversion rates when a lead call comes in! When you get a call off a listing that is in your specialized neighbourhood, you are able to give them valuable information and insights, they didn't already know, or didn't even consider that they *needed* to know, or you may be able to give them intelligent commentary about the surroundings and the amenities that they were not even aware of. Why? Because you are the 'Neighbourhood Specialist! As you increase your talents, strengths, knowledge and confidence; as you gain more and more experience, your ability to convert will increase exponentially. You will eventually work *less* to create a lot m*ore* income. Your dollar per hour will increase exponentially. Your consistency will increase. There is no short-cut to get here, only time and experience can do it. But if you are working on activities that are focused and intentional, you will get to where you need to be faster.

This is my hope for you.

Currency

Would being the Neighbourhood Specialist contribute to better lead conversion rates? Absolutely. As a professional, you build up your currency and your value to others. It's really hard to quantify or calculate, but I will tell you this... your dollar per hour will increase. Your time output versus income will gradually increase and will continue to increase as time goes by. You will increase your currency, but you have to invest in it. You have to be intentional, you have to be consistent and you have to bring value to your neighbourhood first.

Are you convinced? Do we all agree that increasing those three Cs is crucial to building the dream business? **Consistency – Conversion – Currency**. Becoming the Neighbourhood Specialist is a huge part of making that happen. In order to receive consistent cheques, we have put out consistent effort planting seeds and creating value, which will in turn increase our conversion rates. Better conversion rates will then, inadvertently, increase our currency and value and, ultimately, our 'dollars per hour.'

You are intent on OWNING this neighbourhood. You literally want to adopt this neighborhood as your own and you want everyone in the neighborhood to know it. You make the claim and then be true to the claim. This is highly intentional. It's a focused exercise that will take time to master, but you can do it. It will take time, effort and focus. So, remember the old saying, "If it was easy then everyone would be doing it." The truth is that it will absolutely pay off. The business will start to come to you easily and consistently. People will be ATTRACTED to you and will also send business your way.

Over time, this will be one of the best building exercises that you have ever done. Truly.

Let me tell you a story about how being a Neighbourhood Specialist has affected me personally, in my career over the years. In my early real estate days, I had a young couple referred to me from their parents, who I had previously helped. Let's call them Dave and Sarah. They needed to sell their attached townhome and wanted to upgrade to a home in a nice family area with an ample yard and room for a shop. They were a very nice couple. I succeeded in selling their townhome for the right price and found a perfect home that totally met their criteria and budget on the other side of town. I did everything right. This was one of those deals where the client was extremely happy. It was like the stars were totally aligned and everything worked out great for them. Their parents, who had referred them to me, were very happy with how things turned out and Dave and Sarah gave me a great testimonial afterwards. I kept in touch with them. My wife actually got to know Sarah and they bumped into each other once in a while. There was a relationship there. We had experienced success together, and we really connected on a personal level.

But five years later, with all of those things in place, and much to my surprise, they listed their home. But with another real estate agent.

Now, to paint the picture a little more vividly...at that time, I was very aggressive in my marketing. I was everywhere. There was no possible way that they would have forgotten about me. Even though it hadn't been enough, I was in contact with them intermittently; I had done the basic minimum, which was certainly more than some agents get away with. On the flip-side, the real estate agent they listed their home with was just a regular guy. He didn't seem to have much of a presence in the marketplace. His marketing was not great at all, in my opinion. He was older and a nice guy, but not really a hot shot. I couldn't figure it out. I needed to understand why they would decide to deal with someone so "inferior" to me I was a total egomaniac.

So, I called them. I got Dave on the phone and, although he was a bit sheepish, I kept it professional. I didn't want to make him feel bad, I simply wanted to learn why he had chosen this other person. I really thought of Dave and Sarah as 'A' clients. I had had literally zero doubt that they would call me again to do business. None.

This is what Dave told me: "Well, you know, Kelly...sorry... but, you know, I just had to list with this guy. He dropped off calendars and note pads all the time. After a while I got to know him. I just felt compelled to list with this guy."

I was stunned! But then, I thought, *"Well, he earned it... didn't he?"* He did. He absolutely did. He put out more effort than I did in that specific subdivision. I was spending a ton of money on marketing. I had the best website of any other agent out there. I was in the movie theatre with ads. I had two full pages and full color ads in the newspaper every single week. This is a time when the newspaper was a big part of the marketing. Everyone checked out the "Real Estate Review" or the "Real Estate Weekly" paper, which was delivered to every home in our area. I had a team of people to serve my clients. There is no way that these people had forgotten about me. But, I got beat-out by—guess who? — the 'Neighborhood Specialist.' That was a great lesson for me. I am a slow learner. It took me a decade to truly understand the message that I am teaching today.

Here's another key point. Once you start, I suggest that you don't stop. Doing that will kill any momentum that you have built. It's really important to keep the energy flowing. Create systems for your neighborhood , trust in the process and keep moving forward. You will begin to make connections outside of your neighbourhood, and you will deal with people who will refer business to you. Perhaps, you will even meet builders and developers or hit a "vein of business" outside of your target market of buyers and sellers.

I bring this up now, because I don't want you to get tunnel vision, either. There is a delicate balance you must maintain. Sometimes new business, referrals, and new leads and projects will take your business to new places. That's great and exactly what you want. As you connect more dots in your world, the number of people you meet from all walks of life will increase and, as you add more strategic alliances to your database, your business will grow; your influence will, too. Your reputation will grow. With that, your knowledge will grow, about different areas, and different types of real estate business opportunities. This is all good stuff. Be open to that. This is what you want to happen. This is literally how your grow your business.

However, I cannot stress enough how important it is to stay committed to your target market and your target neighbourhood area. This is your bread and butter, the nucleus to your business. Invest your time and effort consistently here and, over the years, it will become your happy place. You know what I mean? Your neighborhood will be like your comfort food, your "Shepherds Pie" or "Warm Beef Stew."

People will begin to accept you as the authority in the area. As you sell more homes in the area, you will be gradually filling up the neighborhood with an army of referral partners. One day, this neighborhood will bring *you* business when the market shifts and you need a little help. All your earlier work will provide you with the repeat business to keep you going in the tough times.

These are YOUR people. This is the place where you can feel comfortable and be yourself. You want these people to know, like and trust you. You are playing the long game here. Remember: If another agent lists a home in this neighborhood, the first business card that should appear on the counter is yours. Picture this: That homeowner—who chose to list with someone else—will get notified of a showing and, when they get home afterwards, they will see that the first showing that happened in their home, was YOU. The Neighborhood Specialist. If that agent fails to sell the home, who do you think they will call next? If that agent holds an open house, in your neighbourhood, you will be holding one and piggy-back off of that person's marketing, as well as your own. You own this neighbourhood. Because it's inevitable, right? It is not realistic to believe that you will be the only agent to list homes in this neighbourhood. But it should bug you. It should feel like a complete stranger just walked into your home and sat down at your couch and put their feet on your coffee table. It should feel like an invasion of your home. This is *your* neighborhood.

There will be outside distractions; other types of business will occasionally take up your time and mental energy because you are a 4X Agent. You are building relationships and receiving referrals all the time. But, but, but...remember to discipline yourself to "keep coming home." Make sure you don't neglect your neighbourhood.

Convinced? Okay.

On the next chapter, we are going to consider some highly effective tactical strategies to execute our plan. We are going to take what you are consistently doing now, every day, and expand on that.

MINDSHARE

Your goal is to become known as the neighbourhood specialist of the area you have adopted. You want to become the authority here. You want everyone who lives here to get to KNOW, LIKE and TRUST you. In my earlier parachute scenario, I reinvented myself as the Mayor of Morningside Park, in Salem, Oregon. Most areas or neighbourhoods have some sort of identifier name based on something like a landmark, a school catchment name or a main road that feeds into the area.Wherever you live, you can go to a city hall, village centre, municipal office or town hall and get a map. Or you can find one on Google. You can get that map blown up and have it on the wall, or in a file, or whatever. But have one in your office. You are activating "Frequency Illusion" by doing this. You are literally absorbing yourself with all of the information that you can get your hands on for this area. You want to be a sponge soaking up as much information as you can about your neighborhood. Suddenly, you will meet people and learn vital details about the neighborhood as if by "happenstance," as you progress along. It is amazing what happens when you begin to focus intently on something. SO...if your particular area doesn't really have a name to identify it, make one up. Why not? If the neighborhood doesn't have a name, YOU name it! Help the people who live there feel the ownership as well. It's a good way to build rapport in the neighbourhood and really solidify you as the Neighbourhood Specialist if you actually create a name for it, if there isn't already one.

You have already embarked on activities in the area and the residents are getting to know you; it is time to make a plan to create relevance, reputation, and rapport with the people in the neighborhood. If you plan ahead and execute the plan before you do anything else, it won't burden you later in the year when you get busy doing business. You will get busy. I am sure of that, but we don't want you to sacrifice the correct execution of this plan just because you got busy. I don't want you to become a victim of your own success. I see ups and downs like this happen *all the time* in real estate.

Remember, we want to eventually enjoy consistency in our business. We want to even out those ups and downs. Invest the time in planning and then it's ultimately easier to execute the plan, when the time comes. I have created a 12-month-blueprint for you to utilize, to help you create a master plan. There are many suggestions on that document to help you come up with a system that works, depending on imagination, support team and budget. Pick and choose what you think can work for you and your neighborhood. I am going to go over suggestions and ideas that you can incorporate into your own businesses.

Some of the suggestions won't apply to you or will be more effective in other neighbourhoods. I know that. You don't have to do it all. You just have to be consistent. Do each suggestion timely and intentionally. I want you to know that you may not see results right away, but I am going to ask you to please trust me on this. If you follow the plan consistently over a period of time, the results will come. This is another version of the "Horsetail Strategy." You are planting seeds underground and you don't know when they are going to pop up and surface, but they will.

Remember the story I told you about being beat out by the Neighbourhood Specialist? I did everything right but failed to get return business from what I thought was an A client. I had a sense of entitlement with that client. But clients are not "your people." You can't brand people like cattle. Don't make the mistakes that I and, frankly, many other agents make. I want you to build your business and solidify it along the way, so that it doesn't take you as long to get to your dream business as it did for me.

Okay. So, I did a little research for you. I went through all twelve calendar months for both the US and Canada and proved my theory that there is something going on every single month of the year that most of the population recognizes and is keyed into. Due to the consumerism in our society, schools, Television, Social Media channels, and Radio stations all contribute to the excitement surrounding these events, so why not ride on the coattails of a larger marketing machine that is already happening. Right? Try to come up with ways to associate yourself with these special days of the year. This is one way to create relevance in the minds of your target neighborhood. You want to get "mindshare." You want to be Top of Mind.

At first, you will have to be very aggressive. I want you to absolutely commit to your plan for 24 months. No excuses. Then you can, maybe, taper off a little bit but, for the first two years or so, you have to be extremely diligent.

The ultimate goal is this: The neighbourhood reads about you, or hears about you, or sees you, or speaks to you or receives something from you (either personally, in email, in social media, through direct mail or in personal drop-offs) a minimum of three to four times per month. Yes. Three or four times a month. That seems like a lot, doesn't it? But this is your neighbourhood. This is your zone, and it represents a lot of sales activity. A large portion of the buyers, 40% of them, shop in this neighbourhood. At any given moment, someone is thinking about buying or selling in this neighborhood. You need to be top of mind. You need to get your name into their brains, and Increase "Mindshare."

I recently read about a survey that was done by an independent marketing firm that works with real estate professionals. Their sole business plan is to get hired to fully develop an agent's brand and create marketing materials for them. They did a test. They surveyed a community and asked them simply that, if they were going to sell, which real estate agent they would call. They kept very good records and quickly began to create a list of the agents who had the most Mindshare in that area. After that, they did another test. They created a "fake" real estate agent and did an eight-week marketing campaign. Now, obviously because it was a fake real estate agent, there was no face to face. There were no open houses, no For Sale signs or anything like that. It was purely a marketing campaign that consisted of mailouts for eight weeks straight, with some clever branding. That's it, mail-outs. These are letters people throw into their recycling, right?

But get this: following the campaign, they called and surveyed the neighborhood again. And would you be surprised to know that this new fake real estate agent was now in the top five?? That's crazy, isn't it?

Mindshare. That's the key. Mindshare. You want to increase your Mindshare constantly. Even when someone throws a mail-out away, they see it. Brand recognition takes place. The first seven throw outs will not necessarily register.

This phenomenon is sometimes referred to as the "Rule of Seven." Actually, the "Rule of Seven" was created in the 1930's and the phrase was coined by the movie industry. It was theorized that, in order to fill the theatres, they had to employ the rule of seven, which states that it takes an average of seven interactions with a specific brand before any commitment to purchase takes place. Though this concept is still somewhat applicable today, we are in a very different world. A poster in a store did a lot more to advertise a movie then than a poster does today. Mail-outs were more effective then. People mostly listened to the radio to get information then. The television was introduced in 1928 and was commercial-free for the first 13 years! It took them quite a while to catch on to the opportunity. 1941 saw the airing of the first TV commercial! It was for a New York watch company called Bulova, and it was a 10 second spot. They paid $9 for that ad, and it was broadcasted just before a Brooklyn Dodgers and Philadelphia Phillies game.

Today, that same 10 second advertisement would cost over $30,000.

In 2018, the company that paid the most for Major League Baseball Advertising spent over $10 Million dollars...if you add up the top 10 advertisers, over $60 Million was spent on TV advertising! That's a lot of money! Finance companies, car companies and communication companies make up some of these top ten corporations spending all this money and what do you think that they are after? The Mindshare of the consumer. Mindshare.

What do you think the odds that someone in their living room watching a baseball game is going to see a TV commercial and then suddenly jump off their couch and go buy a car? Or life insurance. Or switch their cell phone provider. Not likely right?

The large companies know this. They know that the ad is not going to produce a sale today. Yet, they will spend upwards of $4.5 to $10 million per year to make sure that when you DO decide that the time is right for you, that they have planted a seed and possibly tapped into a want, need or desire that connects to their brand.

And that baseball game ad is not all. What about the National Football League? What about the Survivor Finale? What about all of the other places these corporations spend money? It is mind blowing! If these major companies are spending all of this money, just splashing it out there hoping to connect with you, would it make some sense for you to focus your efforts just a little bit more in your own little neighborhood? I think so.

Now, let's look at the various ways we can market to our target group. There are a number of ways to get our message across. We know that people are totally bombarded now with messages coming at them all the time. It's noisy out there. The competition for Mindshare is thousands of times what it was in the 1930s. So, our goal is to get you into the lower category areas. The first four are cold. They require a lot of money and time output for very little return on investment. You want to enjoy a higher Return on Investment, right? You want to increase your currency, by operating with consistency and eventually enjoying increased conversion rates. I want you to think about layering your efforts to increase your Attractor Factor.

THE ATTRACTOR FACTOR

The Attractor Factor takes into account four personal qualities: In order for the people of the neighbourhood to get to know, like, and trust you, you must show them that you are more than simply a "real estate salesperson." You are a...

1. **Service Provider:** You are in the business of helping people buy and sell homes.
2. **Neighbourhood Champion:** You are a person who is passionate and committed to their neighbourhood. You help others see this neighbourhood as a great place to live, eat and play. You are the advocate for this neighborhood.
3. **Capable Specialist:** You are a professional who is seen everywhere in the neighbourhood. You are the "go to" person for information that others can rely upon.
4. **Contributor:** You are a person who is a positive influence in the community.

Okay...so back to the months of the year. We want to make an annual plan. Holidays and other significant events are scattered throughout the months of the year. These days are opportunities to connect with our community. Some of these holidays/events are national, others are provincial. Experiment with tapping into these events to see if there are some business opportunities in them for you.

Utilize the tools found at www.4Xformula.com/attractbook to help you determine how you want to map out the year. Are there any other ways we can make an imprint on the neighbourhood?

Great things will happen once you get your first listing. You'll start to use JUST LISTED flyers. You need to let people know about the new listing. Neighbours will want to know the info. Get the flyers to them first. Touch One. Then let them know about the open house. Maybe you met them at the door to personally invite them...Touch Two. They come to the open house and meet you there...Touch Three. You sell the listing. JUST SOLD flyers go out. Touch Four!! They've already seen your open house signs over the last few weeks. This is already happening!

But here is what normally happens at this point. Once a listing is SOLD and the sign goes down, that's it. Normally. For run-of-the-mill real estate agents. But not for you. This is not the ending. This is just the beginning!! Now you are going to keep your program going throughout the year in various ways, so that your brand stays relevant. You are increasing your Attractor Factor.

Remember when we were talking about the various personality types and how to relate to them? We learned how important it was to be sensitive to the varying degrees of personality types. Well, I would suggest that your neighborhood specialist does the same thing.

I have created a six-point plan in the tools [www.4Xformula.com/attractbook] to show you how you can appeal to all personality types, give value to your community and, ultimately, solidify your Attractor Factor.

The first three items involve new listings, SOLD listings and open houses. The next three items involve getting a little creative. For example, there are various ways to use newsletters. I have seen people put recipes in them. I have seen nice articles written that appeal to the various seasons:

such as spring cleaning, fall landscaping tips, etcetera. I have seen articles with camping hacks for the summertime or barbecuing tips. These are all great ideas. There are myriad articles out there to help you fill a newsletter.

But I would suggest getting even more creative. Involve your business allies. Urge your mortgage partners to write an article, for example. They get their faces and logo on the newsletter, and maybe they can help with cost of printing and distribution. Identify a neighbourhood business you respect and promote them. Then ask that business to have the newsletter sitting in their reception area for a month or two. You might have a coupon for that business in the newsletter. You can ingratiate yourself into the community if you support local businesses. The benefit for you is that there is a better chance of the homeowner keeping the newsletter if it contains value for them, like a coupon, a recipe, mortgage rates or a relevant helpful tip. Maybe get a home inspector to write an article one month, or a notary, a lawyer or a financial planner around tax time. These people can partner with you on these newsletters to help cover the cost and, at the same time, offer value.

The net effect is that the newsletter displays to your neighbourhood that you are aligned with a team of professionals. Every three months, the newsletter could include market report information or a separate mailing, compiled of market sales information pertinent to the neighbourhood. If you have sold and/or listed homes in the area, this is a good place to display that as well. If your stats are better than the average stats, then show *that* in this report. If your "Days on the Market" is lower than the average and your average sale-price-to-list-price ratio is better, this is a great statistic to show on your report. Make the information easy to read and understand. Don't make the stats too complicated; instead, interpret them for the readers. I see stat reports *all the time* and they are often really confusing to the people who are receiving them. They look like investment analysis proformas. Make the statistics friendly looking and easy to understand.

Now, as time goes by, many things are going to happen. You will meet people. It is inevitable. You will have conversations. Throughout all of your efforts, your ultimate goal is to create awareness that you are the "go to person" for real estate information. Full stop. That is what you want people to know. THEN, with that reputation established, you'll have a database of names, phone numbers and email addresses for your Neighbourhood Farm.

There are a lot of ways to achieve this. All of your forms, newsletters, market reports and other correspondence should request for that information. This habit saves paper and also gives people the option to optout at any time, once they are on the email list. Which is okay.

When you meet neighbours at the open houses, or at their door, or when you talk to them on the phone, take a second to ask them if they would prefer to have the newsletters, market reports and notifications of new and sold listings emailed to them instead of receiving your mail-outs. Promise them you will not solicit business from them. You simply want them to know that you are the resource that they can rely upon if they want information. If they already have an agent, that is fine. You are not trying to step on any toes; you simply want to give value to the people who live here. Once you create a Facebook business page and an Instagram page, you can try to find them and get them to follow you. Another idea is to create a mini-website and some social media pages for your neighbourhood. Set rules that restrict negative comments, allowing only positive input about the neighborhood and the people who live in it. This is sensitive, so be careful how you handle this. But a social media page is a great way to communicate to the neighbourhood and, ultimately, it will save you a lot of money and time.

The other way to create more opportunities to meet people is to plan and organize events. There are many ways to create face-to-face opportunities. Your neighbourhood type will influence the varying types of events that you can organize. There is a six-point plan sheet at www.4Xformula.com/attractbook to help you come up with some ideas. If you can organize events and activities that create opportunities for you to meet people, you'll gain Mindshare and increase your Attractor Factor. Your focus is to give value and do something positive for the community; to be a person who cares about the community.

There is usually some sort of set-up involved for events. I would buy a table and a tent, either to create shade or in case of rain. The great thing about a pop-up tent, one that is totally branded with your information on it, is that it creates a powerful presence. You can find 10X10 tents for around $1000 now and get it branded with your name and company. This tent can be used for so many things. You can also lend it out to various people, organizations or events from time to time. All of a sudden, your branding is all over the place. It's a great marketing tool that a lot of people don't really think about.

Okay. Now let's recap everything. What we have been doing from the very beginning is to solidify you as the Neighbourhood Specialist. Right from the Quick Commission Blueprint, through the Get Listings section to Master of the Open House to this point right here, right now. All of the activities that you perform in this neighbourhood are focused on your becoming that person. Adopt the persona. Become that person. Operate intentionally with intense focus, and you will succeed. Don't look for immediate results. Just do the work. Work the plan and you will get the results. Stay consistent. Stay committed. Be creative. Capitalize on *every* opportunity that comes your way.

The truth is, most people know a minimum of three real estate agents and some as many as twelve! But the one they will choose to work with, three out of four times, is the person who is Top of Mind at the moment they enter into the first stage of the buying or selling process. Be that person and you will be there when that moment happens...

Remember the 12 points of Power for the 4X Agent? One of those laws is the Law of Sowing and Reaping. Being Top of Mind is exactly the place where this law applies. It is a law: You reap what you sow. It's that simple. The business will come to you when you 1) make a plan and, 2) work the plan. Then after time, the power of multiplication takes over and you will enjoy the financial benefits. But first, you must commit, make a plan, and work the plan with belief that it will pay off in the future. You will 4X your business.

We have a lot of exciting material ahead in my upcoming three books. The final section in this book is a sneak peek preview of my next book ATTAIN...and that book is all about winning the business, plus tactics and strategies for securing the business. Get great at converting people into raving fan clients and referral sources, and you'll be on your way to creating your own Dream Business.

PREVIEW OF BOOK 2 – ATTAIN

Four Ways to Win

Welcome to the Next Pillar: ATTAIN, Four Ways to Win.

Everything you have done in the ATTRACT section of our course has brought you here. Hopefully, you have had a couple of listing interviews or meetings. If you have already listed some properties, that's great! If you are just beginning and you haven't even figured out how to fill out a listing agreement yet, that's okay, too. Wherever you are in the process, I want to give value to you and walk you through the process, to give you the best chance of success. I want to help you increase your conversion rates and ultimately go into every meeting with the confidence that you will "win" the business. Attract the Opportunity and then Attain the Business. There should never be any doubt in your mind.

Before we get into the actual tactics and strategies of ATTAIN, it is important to understand that there is a process to winning business in real estate. How do 4X'ers interpret "Winning the Business"? There are actually **Four Ways to Win**, because there are four basic stages that buyers and sellers are at when you come into contact with them. This is a really important facet of building a real estate business. If you understand these four stages, you can figure out how to spend your time and prepare for your meetings appropriately, with the understanding of the potential outcomes from every meeting. How you can activate, win, or salvage business from all four potential outcomes is by using The 4X Formula strategy to minimize the casualties along the way. This is the distinction that makes 4X Agents different from the rest.

The Four Stages that I have come across in my business are these:

1. The NOW people: There is urgency here; motivation is high.
2. The SOON people: They're ready to make a move but need to create a workable plan. Not so urgent, but in motion.
3. The FUTURE people: They're thinking about making a future life change but are presently only in the planning stages.
4. "Only a Seller IF": This is a scenario-based buyer or seller. Let's call them **UNICORNS**. We will talk about Unicorns later.

You can easily see the difference above. Let's look at each of these types of people in their various stages.

The **NOW** People

We love the **NOW** people. The **NOW** people can be put into three sub-groups:

1) The *RELATIONSHIP* client is ready to rock!

If they are a return client, or a friend/family member, and have called you up and are in a "giddy up and go" mentality, then it's 'go' time. Rock and roll. You have some foundational knowledge about them. You already have a relationship and rapport with these people. You are working from an accelerated state. This is great. As you move through your business, you will get more and more of these relationship clients from your own database and referral network. This is the best and least stressful client. The lowest-hanging fruit.

2) The *STRANGER* client is calling you and they are in an urgent state-of-mind.

It is important to ensure that it is *you,* who are going to be helping them. They may be in 'go' mode, but you may be competing for the business with another real estate agent. If you are fairly new in the business, then this is most likely the bulk of your business. This client is in this **NOW** stage mentally, and somehow you have made yourself top-of-mind to make the connection.

Congratulations, you achieved mindshare by getting to stage six or seven in the Stages of Contact! They might be a person who lives in your neighborhood and are already convinced that you are the best choice; they want the same service you gave their neighbor last month. If so, that is fantastic...your efforts have paid off! Mission accomplished. This is exactly what your goal is, so go into "go mode"!

However, you aren't necessarily privy to their more intimate details. You may still need to learn more about them. It's very important that you don't skip over the details. You need to understand their plans, the reason for the urgency, what their motivation is.

The same goes for the RELATIONSHIP clients. A lot of agents will get caught up in the urgency and simply jump in, unprepared, and hope to discover these elements along the way. This will ultimately frustrate the clients because they won't have the proper advice and in so doing, may have false expectations for the agent. This can be dangerous, as an agent may be damaging a good reputation that they have built in their neighbourhood.

It is a critical component to your overall game plan for this neighbourhood that you create advocates and referral sources, and quickly build a great reputation within your target zone market. Remember, reputation is the #1 reason people select their real estate agent. Neighbourhood knowledge is important, but in comparison to REPUTATION, there is a landslide difference. Reputation is huge. That is why it is so important to stick to your process. The "Pre-Listing Prep Worksheet" is a tool that is to be used in ALL circumstances so that you stick to the plan and keep yourself in your lane and ensure that you don't miss the details. This will help you preserve your reputation by leaving less room for error.

In this Pillar, we will also be talking to you about the buyer process, as well. Don't shortcut this. You'll need to remember the steps and gain a clear understanding of how to serve these people well. You may still be competing for the business in this scenario and we need to set things up for you to win. You already have a high percentage chance of winning, because you are being given a chance.

3) The *FIRE & FIZZLE* client.

Some people from the NOW and STRANGER groups will fall into his group, believe it or not. The 4X Agent process will help to alleviate the chance of getting caught in this trap. I have seen it happen many times to other agents, and I have had it happen to me many times over the years. It will likely happen to you, too. It's okay. Just be aware of it. Believe it or not, sometimes your client needs to go through this to prepare them for the process. They may have to learn a hard lesson. Then after you go through it with them, they will learn that they trust you. You will experience frustration here, for sure. But this is actually a good thing, in the long-term of your relationship. Here is an example of this scenario happening.

You get a phone call from your client and they are in a state of urgency and excitement. *"Hey Sharon, we found the perfect place today. We went to an open house over on XYZ street and this is the place. This is the home we want.*

need you to write up the offer and get our place listed on the market as soon as possible! When can we get together?"

Don't overlook the warning signs here. The clients are posing some essential questions for you: What do we know? What don't we know? What do we need to know? They're counting on you.

Here are some more examples of questions that you'll need to have answers for, before you move forward. Remember, this is just an example of what *my* mind would go through.

- ☐ Do they have to sell in order to buy? Is there no other way?
- ☐ What are the odds of their house selling in time to make a deal on this place that they want?
- ☐ Is their motivation to sell tied onto this "dream house" only? If they can't get this place, is it all for naught? Fizzle.
- ☐ Is their house ready to go onto the market?
- ☐ Is their financing in order? What numbers have they given their mortgage lender to calculate the potential for success?
- ☐ Is their expectation for selling based on the absolute best-case scenario, or is there some room to make the plan come together?
- ☐ Are they realistic about the price expectation for their home? Will it sell within 30 days?
- ☐ Would the seller accept a "subject to sale" offer?
- ☐ Is the property they are excited about priced well? Or is it priced too well? Is there a possibility that multiple offers could eliminate the chances for success, if they have to sell to buy? OR...Is it totally over-priced?

See all ways that a FIZZLE could occur?

The Fire & Fizzle group of The NOW People can be risky. The Fizzle can hurt the relationship sometimes, so you have to be careful in how you handle things. Be their advocate and trusted advisor and fight for them. You may not achieve the result on this first try but, as a team, you will make it work on the second try.

Though it seems that, at first, you are a victim of the Fire & Frizzle group's "frantic-ness," the work that you do and the advice that you give them will produce fruit at a later date. The best thing to do is to understand their motivation. You have learned what gets them fired up. You didn't get paid here, but if you operate properly, you will get paid eventually from the relationship.

Next are the SOON and the FUTURE categories.

Essentially, what you need to know is that your relationship with the SOON and FUTURE people needs to be nurtured. These people are tied to a different type of motivation and that motivation hasn't intensified yet to the right boiling point. That is perfectly fine. Because these people are tied into motivation, we will touch on this after the UNICORNS. We have to be aware of the people who are looking for UNICORNS, so that we can determine if the SOON and FUTURE people are not part of that group.

The "ONLY-IF..." People, The Unicorns

Let's talk about Unicorns. These people are very clear about their criteria. They know what they want. Most of the time, they are able to communicate that desire to you, very well. Sometimes, because of this, we agents end up spending a lot of time looking for the seemingly impossible.

Be very careful about the Unicorns. If you choose to work with them, it must be a conscious decision. You know what you are in for. They are "only selling if..." and they are "only buying if..." They are totally scenario driven. The IF is usually a big IF. Remember, I am just helping you identify the various client types, so you can decide where to spend your time.

Sometimes you can pull it off, and the pieces come together. It is worth it to list their home, if you feel that you can attract at least two buyers from that home. If it comes together, then you meet your goal. Usually, the Unicorn is a buyer on your list who is searching for an unusual piece of property. It's a unique scenario; the price is not really achievable. They probably know that what they are looking for is hard to find and that's why they are utilizing your services. They may be the patient because the scenario, or ideal, is what — drives the motivation. That's okay. But if you determine that the process is eating up a lot of time and energy, and the likelihood of success is minimal, you might want to let this one go. I would still keep them on my list and do a little check-in every once in a while and send them some listings that have some sort of potential. But that's it. Don't waste too much time on Unicorns. Make sure that all of your **NOW** and **SOON** people are taken care of first. If you find that perfect scenario property, then the Unicorns they turn into **NOW** people. The good thing about Unicorns is that they usually move pretty fast.

If you determine right from the beginning that what the Unicorns are looking for is too difficult to find, then refer them to someone else or let the lead dissipate. It's not worth wasting your mental space, if it doesn't pay out. Remember, you want to increase your dollar-per-hour. The key here is to recognize the Unicorn person and operate with that knowledge. See what happens, but don't let them take away from your business development activities for **FUTURE** clients and your ability to serve your **NOW** and **SOON** clients.

Sometimes, a **NOW** person may only be an "**Only IF**" person. If these people have gravitated from the 2nd group of **SOON** people, then you may have a lot of these answers already and some prep has already been done. This is most likely the case. If their perfect scenario doesn't come together as they'd hoped, they fall into the SOON category and they simply have to get their "ducks in a row" to get ready for the next opportunity. Don't lose them, if this scenario doesn't work out. Get them into prep mode with a plan that will get them on track. There is usually a better opportunity around the corner, when they are properly prepared to handle it. This is what I mean by leaving no casualties behind.

Remember, a 4X agent builds relationships; a 4X agent operates with intention; a 4X agent is always in control. The clients need to feel that from you. You need to ask questions to get them to slow down and think about all aspects of the process.

We always talk about planting seeds in this book and in my course. This is another part of the "Horse-tail" strategy. You are always seed-planting. If you become a master of this, you will always have people moving into the NOW stage of Four Ways to Win. You can't control when this happens. You can't control or manipulate people into entering the NOW stage. Accept this. But you *can* control your relationship with them while they are sitting in limbo between the SOON and NOW stages. You can be a person of value to these people. Keep sending them pertinent information, on a consistent basis, towards preparing them for that moment when the time is right. Keep yourself Top-of-Mind with these people so when they do land on something and move from a seemingly "dormant" state, to a state of "giddy-up and go," then everyone is ready to move forward with confidence and decisions will be made quickly.

The SOON and FUTURE people are driven by something that will be motivating them. The SOON people are usually in some sort of preparation mode. Personally, I am thinking that they are going to be activating the plan within the next 40 to 120 days or so. That is what I mean by SOON. We are slightly active. We are keeping them updated on Market Activity. We may be visiting them at their home periodically to chat. We may even go out and look at some homes once in a while to keep them abreast of the market. I am hoping that they see something that may get them to increase the urgency to get into the NOW category.

The FUTURE Category of people is similar to the SOON people, but they are most likely waiting for some sort of life event to happen. It could be tied into their job advancement or possibly retirement. It could be connected to something to do with their children, older family members. They may be waiting for funds from an investment of some sort. Sometimes, it is much more emotional than that. Perhaps they have lived at their property for over 35 years and there are many memories that they are holding onto. They know that the work to maintain the property is killing them physically but they just can't seem to move on. Getting them to mentally turn the corner can be tough, and it is a delicate process. There are many factors that could be holding them back. Alternatively, there are possibly, many factors that will cause them to put the pedal down and accelerate their plans. Think about these people this way. Remember it is all about the plan. Do you remember the plan that you had a discussion about? Is there something in the plan that you can find a new motivation for? Is there something about the market activity that can create an advantage for them if they make a move now? Is timing crucial right now?

One thing to understand about motivation is this: there are usually **two reasons that drive it.** Someone is **moving towards** something that they want, or someone is **moving away** from something. Sometimes the "moving away" from something is the stronger motivator and will produce urgency. For example: a) the client has a home with lots of stairs and they just went through knee surgery and need a one-level home; or b) The clients have a horrible neighbor, or c) they live in an area where the daily commute is over an hour long. In each of these cases, they want to move away from something, and they have a picture in their mind of what they want to move to.

Now, let's talk about Decision Drivers. Before anyone makes a decision to move toward or away from something, they first need to help remove any obstacles.

Obstacles to Decision Making.

As a 4Xer, you will be an expert on the obstacles to decision making. Here is a working list that will help you understand your clients better:

1) Confusion about the process

2) Lack of confidence

3) Lack of clarity

4) Fear of making the wrong decision

At least one of these nagging concerns will be in the back of the client's mind. Our goal is to help them navigate through these obstacles and get them to a place of clarity, confidence, and fearlessness. Once they get there, a decision will be made.

But you, the agent, need to get clear first. If *you* don't have clarity, how are you going to help them go in the direction that *they* want to go? If *you* aren't confident in the scenario, then how will *they* be? So, how do we get there? By seeking to understand. By asking the correct questions. By being mindful of the client's frame of reference. By cutting through the confusion. By breaking down the challenges and working your way to solutions. We need to understand the client's perfect scenario before we can find it for them.

There are a few different ways to approach this. We can use the **Let's Pretend Approach:**

"Ok, Bob and Mary, let's pretend everything works out exactly the way you want it to. Walk me through that perfect scenario."

Then, listen very intently and make notes. Doing this will uncover the client's hot buttons, fears, and motivations. This strategy works for both buyers and sellers. You will learn a lot from this question, because it is an intimate one. What you will learn, is one of two things: They have really thought it through, or they haven't really thought it all the way through. This is where you learn about their confusions. You'll uncover their fears, which even they may only be discovering, while also figuring out their perfect scenario.

Do most people, who have a specific budget, ever find the absolute perfect ten out of ten home? No, very rarely. In the process, it is important to talk to your buyer clients to prepare them and help them come to the realization that it is okay if the home is not 100% perfect. For example, try something like this:

"As you can see at this price point, you may have to prioritize the things that you really want in a home. If we can get seven or eight out of ten, then that would be fantastic. We have found that sometimes, the really important things that were in the top three, end-up being in the bottom three, as we move along the process. Funny, but it's important to see enough product to help you discover that for yourselves. We just have to be open to those possibilities."

See how we handle that? We give them permission to be flexible. We are telling them that they may not get ten out of ten, and that it's okay. We will always do our best, as agents, but to believe that we can always achieve 100% for people is not realistic. Do you see how knowing this can help you in the buyer process?

Okay, but what about the selling process? Do sellers always get the exact closing dates they want? Do they always get the exact price that they were hoping for? Does it always happen as soon as they want it to happen? What percentage, out of 100 deals, are going to go 100% perfect? I bet less than 5%. In my experience of doing thousands of real estate transactions, I know that 100% satisfaction does not happen very often. So, it makes sense to address and prepare the client for this. They need to feel that they are achieving their best-case scenario, even if things aren't 100% perfect. We have to help them understand the "non-negotiables" and where "there is a little give" in the overall, end result. Ultimately, this will reduce friction. Managing expectations is part of our job.

Speak to the clients about potential future challenges. There are many ways to do this. One way is to ask them to picture their best-case scenario. Ask them simple questions. I like to call this "The Process." I want to know how they see the process going. Here are some examples:

"Okay, Linda, I think I am beginning to understand how to help you. Can you take a quick moment and just run through with me, how you see this process going from beginning to end?"

"How do you see this playing out?"

"Let's walk through the process together, so that I can clearly understand how I can help you get there."

The magical thing about doing The Process is that you are causing everyone to think it through and consider all of the angles. You are moving the scenario from one side of the brain to the other, from the emotional to the logical side. Reasoning kicks in. Discoveries will happen. Everyone will get on the same page and the appropriate expectations will be realized. You will see where the holes are in their expectations and you can gently go over those things with them. They will accept your advice here, because they most likely haven't even thought of it. They may even have an 'aha' moment, *"...crap, I never thought of that!"*

Experience will be your teacher here, but as time goes by and your experience grows, The Process will become a great asset to relationship-building with your clients.

It's unavoidable; eventually, something will hit the fan. Little blips or hiccups will happen. It's best to address those possibilities now, in the early stages. What happens most of the time, is the "issue" or "challenge" will hit later into the process. If we aren't prepared for the possibility when that happens, it will feel more like a blockage to the process if nobody has brought it up before it happens. It will feel like a bigger problem than it really is. It is hard to manage the emotions. The risk is that it will kill the excitement and the momentum. A bunch of time, effort, energy, and emotional energy will be expended and potentially cause the fizzle to happen. I would rather the fizzle to occur at the beginning, than at this later stage.

But if you deal with the stumbling blocks early in the process, then the worst-case scenario has already been identified. The clients begin to get clarity, and maybe there is a detail that needs to be handled before moving forward. That's okay; there is clarity in the details. Let's deal with them first and then move forward confidently. The beauty is that you are still moving forward, still in motion. That is more positive than being halted, mentally hitting a wall, or having to go backwards for a while. This is true for every single scenario. Be the navigator. Ensure that everyone is prepared for the process.

We have broken down the Four Ways to Win! People measure the win when they are writing offers. If you write an offer every single day, you are definitely "Winning the Day" aren't you? Selling properties and getting commission cheques is easy to measure; we call that the LAG measure. Remember Goal Setting? The LEAD measures are the LEAD Development aspects of your business. You need to be conscious of where your leads are in their process, at all times. Tracking this is part of your day. Use your LEAD Tracker, your Contact Form and your Pre-Listing Prep sheets to help track and keep you Top-of-Mind and also to ensure that these LEADS stay top-of-mind with you, in your daily and weekly activities. Make sure there are no holes in the bucket. This is a habit that a lot of real estate agents miss out on. Plant seeds, every single day, and you are winning the day.

MEASURES CHECKLIST:

- ☐ How many people did you meet or talk to for the first time about real estate?
- ☐ How many people did you touch base with, to nurture business?
- ☐ How many people did you show houses to this week?
- ☐ How many people did you meet with, to talk about a plan for selling their home this week?
- ☐ How many Open Houses are you doing per month?
- ☐ How many people attend your Open Houses?
- ☐ What is your lead conversion rate?
- ☐ How many hot buyers are on your list right now? (It should take you no more than one second to answer this question)
- ☐ How many listings do you have right now?
- ☐ How many are in the hopper for the next few months? (SOON and FUTURE and even UNICORNS)

You will know these numbers because that is what your daily activities are all about: knowing the numbers. Knowing your business. Knowing where things need to be propped up. Knowing where you are on track. Knowing when you are succeeding.

This is getting exciting, isn't it? This concludes this first chapter of my next book, ATTAIN.

CONCLUSION AND WHAT'S NEXT?

Thank you, Reader. Thank you for continuing to read this book to the end. The Real Estate Industry thanks you and your office thanks you and eventually I hope your family and loved ones thank you, when you begin to produce the results in your life and create a consistent business. The lifestyle that can be created from a good solid, consistent real estate business is amazing. My wife, Nicole and I have enjoyed a wonderful life and we are thankful for the opportunities presented to us in the Real Estate Industry. My hope for you is that you create a database of clients who are fiercely loyal to you and referrals become a common theme in your daily business life. Remember to work every day. Work. Every day. On all parts of your business. Read your WHY Worksheet and your GOALS every day. Keep your mind sharp. Become a master of your craft. Become a master conversationalist. Remember to focus on all areas of your business and keep track of everything. Stats are super important. Your personal statistics are your personal statistics. You don't have to share them with others for bragging purposes. It is valuable information for you to understand the metrics of your business so that you can improve constantly.

I encourage you to take this information and implement it into your life and your business. Another way to ensure that is to go to 4Xformula.com and become a member. Membership has its privileges. As an owner of this book, I have given you free access to the tools that I have created from over 2 decades of experience. I knew that just simply talking about how to create systems was not enough. I had to give you the ability to implement systematically. You may not choose to utilize everything that I have created, I understand that. If you go through the course and become a member, you will re-enforce the principals even further, and begin to take advantage of the further lessons before those books come out. There are already more lessons being loaded into the ATTAIN section of the course even before this book covering the ATTRACT section of the course is completed and released.

This section of the course – ATTRACT – and ultimately this book, has taken you on a journey. This journey has taken you through all of the foundational aspects, to generate the opportunity to meet Buyers and Sellers and future prospects. We covered how "mini-successes" build belief. We established that BELIEF is the absolute crucial element, to achieving success. Belief is the key to it all. I hope that seed of Belief is now germinating to overtake those little seeds of doubts that may be in your mind, even after reading this book. Continue to cultivate and grow those seeds of belief and eventually those seeds of doubt will die and wither away.

Now, I am certain that if you perform the activities contained within this book, that you will ATTRACT people to you and you will create opportunities for listings and to meet buyers.

In ATTAIN, I teach you how to WIN the business. It's that simple.

ATTAIN is all about handling those meetings. Now that you are face to face with these people, what skills are required? What strategies are required? How do you create certainty? How do you create the BELIEF that you will WIN the business just about every single time you get an opportunity to meet someone?

The Listing Meeting is first. We cover every single detail for that critical meeting, in ATTAIN.

How do you prepare for a listing meeting after you have taken to the time to fill out the Pre-Listing Prep Sheet and booked the appointment?

How do you properly prepare the file? What information do you need? What research is necessary?

(I will give you a hint – there is more to it than simply a CMA.)

How do you stand out from the crowd? How can you be different? How can you present yourself so that the Seller picks you – every time, if you are competing for the listing?

I have a fool proof strategy for that, that I personally use in my business right now. I call it The Schedule A. This is the most powerful tool in your "presentation" and I have never heard anyone talk about it. I have taught it to many people, and it is a "no-fail" strategy to win listings. This lesson alone will change your life.

By the way, I call it a "Listing Conversation" rather than a "Listing Presentation." Imagine having this level of confidence! You are not going to meet someone to "present" or "make a proposal" and then HOPE that they pick you. You are going over to someone's home, to have a Conversation about Listing their home. That is the difference. That is the distinction.

The 4XFormula Strategy is the create 4 commission cheques out of every listing opportunity. That is the goal every time. Winning the Listing is part of that strategy. The second part of that strategy is to ATTRACT and ATTAIN two Buyers to sell homes to.

This Listing now becomes a tool to leverage more Leads for you. In the beginning, you employ the 3 "L's" – LEADS, LEADS, LEADS. LEADS are the most important factor. But after ATTRACT and as you move into ATTAIN, the 3 "L's" change to LEADS – LISTINGS – LEVERAGE. The word LEVERAGE will change as you progress in your business. But in this phase of your business development, the word LEVERAGE is entirely centered around – ATTRACTING more business to ATTAIN from the business that you are in the middle or working on. I call it "4Xing" your business. Utilize the power of multiplication. 4X your efforts.

Buyers are guaranteed commission cheques. Buyers are the most economical and profitable business. You are forced to spend marketing dollars to get your listings sold. You may be paying for MATTERPORT specialists, and designing brochures, professional photographers, and Videographers, Stagers, and other service providers to market a home appropriately to get it SOLD. But that is just one fourth of the result that you want to accomplish with this investment in this listing. If you sell that listing without attracting Buyers then it is my opinion that you have squandered opportunity.

When you "market a home" instead of "listing a home" you are Marketing to ATTRACT buyers to buy that home – right? So, who are you marketing to? Buyers!! Yes Buyers!!

When you list a home. You are listing it on the MLS system. The system of cooperation. To allow other Real Estate Agents to sell that listing. Great. That is a guaranteed sale. That is the a "no-brainer." Anyone can do that. It takes zero creativity or intelligence to achieve that result. One deal, and maybe two if that seller needs to buy a home.

As a 4X Agent, you want to 4X your business. You MARKET Homes to not only "sell" the listing to the right buyer, but also to ATTRACT and ATTAIN at least 2 Buyers off of the marketing for that home, AND, while you are marketing that home, you are planting seeds for more listings in that neighborhood. In addition to that, there is a high likelihood that one of those Buyers has something to sell. Let's quantify this theory...

Let's pretend that each commission cheque is $5000.

Let's add up a 4X Agents potential income from 1 Listing

1. List the home and sell it $5000
2. Sell that Seller a Home $5000
3. Attract 2 Buyers who buy Homes $10,000
4. One of those Buyers needs to sell a home $5000
5. List and Sell a Home in the Neighborhood $5000
6. Sell that person a Home $5000
7. Attract 2 Buyers who buy Homes $10,000
8. One of those Buyers needs to sell a home $5000

And the cycle keeps going and going and going.... that is the 4X formula at work!!!

There is over $50,000 from one listing generating Leads! It took one good lead to cause this cycle. How is your level of BELIEF doing now? How much is 1 Listing worth? Well, in this case over $50,000. Is it worth the effort to plan an Open House properly? Is it worth it to make sure the neighborhood knows about your listing? Is it worth it to take the time to view every listing in your target market area?

Is it worth it to go to 4XFormula.com and become a Member to learn how to WIN the LISTING every time you have an opportunity for an appointment?

Learn my secret strategies that I have never seen taught to WIN the listing every time you have a chance to have a conversation with someone about selling their home. Your next 10 Listings have the potential to turn into 40 Deals! Check it out. You owe it to yourself to invest in your business.

I hope you also take advantage of my FREE Content:

- PODCAST: 4X RADIO – 4X Formula Real Estate training – find me on Spotify, Apple, Google Play, Anchor and all of the other apps for podcasting.
- YOUTUBE: Look for 4X Formula Real Estate in the search bar.
- Free FACEBOOK Group: The Real Estate Agents Learning Centre
- Find me on Clubhouse: @4xcoachkelly
- Find me on LinkedIn: Look for Kelly Johnston 4XFormula Real Estate
- Find me on Facebook: kellyjohnston.training
- Find me on Instagram: @realestate.with.kelly
- Find me on Twitter: 4x_real

Please do not give this book away. Keep this book as your workbook. Make notes. Highlight the points that you need to remember and use it as your reference guide to keep you focused. When ATTAIN comes out then you can add it to your collection. If you want to share the information, please encourage others to purchase the book. It is so easy to go online and order books now. Feel free to take a picture of yourself and post it online and tag me in the photo. That would be much appreciated!

Take care,

Kelly Johnston

TOOLS

Reminders of Homework & Tools to utilize:

WAITING LIST

- Realtor® Self Assessment Form

FOUNDATIONS

- WHY Worksheet
- GOAL Sheet in the FRAME
    - LEAD Sheet
    - Goal Setting Worksheet
    - Goal Tracker

BONUS MATERIAL

- MINDSET Mastery – Do a personality profile test. (Affiliate)?
- QUICK Commission Blueprint – DO Worksheet to determine Target Market

ATTRACT:

- **Art of Conversation** - Engage people in every interaction
    - Contact Card
- **GET LISTINGS:**

- Scripts – Expiries – *(Video 1)*
  - Meet at letter drop off
  - Phone call after letter drop off
    - Letter to Expired's
    - Script to Expired's
    - Letter to Expired 40%
    - Script to Expired 40%
- Scripts – FSBO – *(Video 2)*
  - Drop off Letter
  - Phone call introduction
  - Phone call follow-up after viewing home
    - Letter for FSBO
    - Script for FSBO
- Mind Trigger Questions FOR Lead Spreadsheet – *(Video 3)*

- **Preparation HABITS**
- **Pre-LISTING PREP**
  - Pre-Listing Interview form.
- **Master of the Open House**
  - Open House CHECKLIST
  - Open House Sign in Sheet
  - "How to get ready for an Open House" brochure for seller
  - 7 Stages of Contact
  - Neighborhood Invite Script
- **Neighborhood Specialist**
  - 12 Month Farming Plan
  - 6 Layers of Contact
  - Neighborhood Partners

Here are some of the tools you will have access to at www.4Xformula.com/attractbook.

Copies of all the TOOLS mentioned in this book for your reference. Go get your full sized PDF copy at 4XFormula.com/attractbook

Manufactured by Amazon.ca
Bolton, ON

25165702R00153